Marrying Later, Marrying Smarter

also by Tracy Cabot

Letting Go: A Personal Action Program to Overcome a Broken Heart

How to Make a Man Fall in Love with You

How to Keep a Man in Love with You Forever

Manpower: How to Win the Woman of Your Dreams

Marrying Later, Marrying Smarter

TRACY CABOT, Ph.D.

McGRAW-HILL PUBLISHING COMPANY

New York   St. Louis   San Francisco
Toronto   Hamburg   Mexico

1 2 3 4 5 6 7 8 9 DOC DOC 9 5 4 3 2 1 0

ISBN 0-07-009509-4

Library of Congress Cataloging-in-Publication Data

Cabot, Tracy.
    Marrying later, marrying smarter / by Tracy Cabot.
        p.   cm.
    IBSN 0-07-009509-4
    1. Mate selection—United States.   2. Marriage—United States.
    I. Title.
    HQ801.C255   1990
    646.7'7—dc20
                                                                89-49589
                                                                CIP

Book design by Eve Kirch

To my husband, Marshall Whitfield

CONTENTS

ACKNOWLEDGMENTS

This book would not have been written without the help of many people. Among those I'd like to extend my thanks to are:

my agents, Pam Bernstein and Robert Gottlieb of the William Morris Agency, for their direction and support;

my editor, Anne Sweeney, for her insightful guidance;

my mother, Ruth Blank, for her encouragement;

my father, Ben Blank, for his thoughtful suggestions;

my dear friends, Elaine Stansfield, Helen Cherry, Bernadette McNulty-Krugman, Margo Kaufman, Darlene Hayes, Laura Singer-Gans, Jennifer Sharlit, Terri Mayo, Ruth Halcomb, and Susan Bloch, who unselfishly shared of their time and their lives;

my clients and members of Great Expectations, whose success at finding love later in life inspired this book.

A PERSONAL NOTE FROM
THE AUTHOR

When I married for the first time—at age forty-two—everyone was surprised. I was thrilled and delighted, fulfilled and relieved.

As an older bride, I was able to appreciate my marriage in a way no teenage bride ever could. I didn't feel as if I were giving up a great, fun, single life. I'd been single long enough to know that after the first ten or twenty years, dating begins to mean just another fattening dinner you can live without.

I'd been single long enough to know the pain of being alone in a coupled world. There's nothing more excruciating than watching happy couples together when you're alone. You're supposed to feel good for them, but it's almost impossible to stop those nagging thoughts: "What's she got that I haven't got?" "How come nobody loves me?" Usually followed by, "There must be something wrong with me," especially when your friends' kids are in high school and you're still single.

For the past five years, my workshops and private practice have been filled with women and men discovering how to change destructive love behaviors into healthy ones, and learning to find someone to love for the rest of their lives.

Most intriguing for me personally have been those over-thirty women clients who considered themselves hopeless, who had gotten to that "I guess I'll never get married" stage I recognized so well. These women were certainly not losers. They were attractive, bright, and successful, with lots of love to give the right man, yet they felt doomed to spend their lives alone.

Although these single women were all different as individuals, I began to see that they had similar patterns of thinking and behavior that were sabotaging their relationships. Invariably, my advice would involve changing these patterns, and soon my client would succeed in finding the man she wanted. I became fascinated with the larger question: Could these "failure patterns" I kept seeing be the reason so many otherwise successful women over thirty hadn't been able to find a lasting love relationship?

Two years ago I decided to test my theory through an in-depth study of thousands of men and women who were members of Great Expectations, a nationwide video dating service. Based on surveys, videotapes, personality profiles, and individual interviews with those women over thirty who got married and those who didn't, it became clear that those who were *not* successful showed exactly the same "failure patterns" as my clients were showing.

Even more important, the original tapes and interviews of the women who found someone, fell in love, and got married showed the exact *opposite* patterns of thinking and behavior. They had "patterns of success" from the beginning.

In *Marrying Later, Marrying Smarter* you will learn about these patterns—which cause failure and which bring success in finding lasting love. You'll meet dozens of women who have changed their relationship failure patterns often against all odds—women like Helga, whose crazed boyfriend almost bit off her nose, and Ellie, who nearly went from a Park Avenue apartment to a prison cell because her boyfriend was an art forger, and Ruth, whose husband cheated on her continuously for ten years. All these women went on to marry wonderful men. Their experiences are real. Only their names have been changed to maintain confidentiality.

My studies and the true stories of these women show that you don't have to be young to find true love, nor do you have to be gorgeous, have a terrific personality or be great in bed. You don't need a track record of successful relationships. You don't need lots of money or connections. What you need is an open mind, a willing heart and the persistence to go after what you want.

So if you've been thinking about giving up—don't. There are lots and lots of men out there looking for someone just like you. You're not too old. You can beat the odds and find a husband at any age.

By following my proven plan, you can dramatically increase your chances of being married in the near future. Simply by changing the way you think about the problem and your approach to finding men, you can find the right man, fall in love and get married.

The *Marrying Later, Marrying Smarter* plan consists of recognizing and stopping any destructive relationship patterns you've developed, replacing them with healthy relationship patterns and leading your heart with your head rather than with other parts of your anatomy.

Marrying Later, Marrying Smarter is for you if you've put off marriage and now that you're ready it seems as if there's nobody to marry.

Marrying Later, Marrying Smarter is for you if you've had one or more unsuccessful marriages and now you're ready to have a smarter marriage.

Marrying Later, Marrying Smarter is for you if you're ready to stop jumping through hoops for every man you start to date.

Marrying Later, Marrying Smarter is for you if you are ready to put aside your preconceived ideas of how romance should happen and take an active role in *making* it happen.

CHAPTER ONE

An End to Endless Dating

Don't worry. It's not too late! It wasn't too late for me, or for the hundreds of women I've helped to get married, and it's not too late for you.

When I married for the first time, in my forties, statistics reported in a national magazine said that I had a better chance of getting killed by a terrorist. I know what it's like to have people ask, "How come a nice girl like you isn't married?" I was fed up with go-nowhere relationships, singles' bars, anxious parties and constantly facing the stigma of being unmarried in a coupled society. I was uncomfortable being the only one without a mate at family gatherings, and I was disappointed because that intimate connection with another human being had eluded my grasp. I was lonely, and I was worried about spending the rest of my life alone.

I'd still be single if I hadn't discovered several important new principles, starting with a big difference in the way I met my husband. I didn't simply flirt at a party or let him pick me up in a bar. I *chose* him, according to the *Marrying Later, Marrying Smarter* success plan.

To marry successfully, I had to replace the relationship failure patterns that were keeping me single with success patterns. You, too, may have relationship failure patterns that keep you single.

Failure Pattern 1: Waiting to Be Chosen Instead of Choosing

How did you choose the last person you fell in love with? Did you select him because of something you knew about him? Or did your eyes suddenly meet across a crowded room and you knew it was love, just like in the movies?

Did you run into him over the brussel sprouts at the market or over the bench press machine at the health club? These accidental meetings, although they can be fun, rarely end in marriage for older, very particular singles.

Carol, a lawyer, came to me when she was thirty-six. A tall blonde with big brown eyes and a knockout figure, she could have had any man she wanted. Looking at her, it was hard to imagine that she'd ever have a problem with men.

"I don't understand it. I meet men all the time. But there's always something wrong with them. They're too weird, they're withholders or they're just unwilling to get close. Even when I meet a nice man and he seems to like me a lot, it never comes to anything. Maybe I'll never find the right man. I'm really getting worried.

"I date all the time, and lately I've been going on ski trips and having a wonderful time, but I want more. I'm tired of dating. I want to get married and have a family, and soon it's going to be too late."

Carol always found men the easy way. She didn't have to do anything. Men were simply drawn to her beauty—which meant she had lots of men, but they all wanted her as an armpiece or for sex, not because they were attracted to who she really was. Few were interested in a long-term relationship, and the ones who were interested didn't meet her standards.

I asked Carol to write down the first names of the last three men she'd gone out with, and how she met them. Elliot, a lawyer, still ached from his own recent divorce and only wanted to have fun. They met in her office building. Sebastian, a well-known member of the investment community, was a fifty-two-year-old bachelor who lived with his mother. Carol met him at a party. John, a college professor who had decided to give up teaching and become a screenwriter, was more interested in his career than in marrying anyone. They met at a ski show.

We analyzed how those relationships had started, and how they'd progressed. Then we looked for any common thread in the relationships. It quickly became clear. The men had absolutely nothing in common except that they had all picked Carol. *She hadn't chosen them*. In fact, it turned out that she had never chosen a man, even once in her life.

I explained to her that since she obviously knows more about what she wants and needs than a stranger at a party, she should begin choosing men instead of being chosen by them. Instead of meeting the next man by accident, she should qualify him to ensure that her needs would be met. So far, only the men's needs were being met. They got an attractive, fun date, a ski and tennis pal and a dinner companion who made interesting conversation, but Carol's needs for a committed relationship were being overlooked.

Carol cautiously began to think about choosing. "It makes sense, but I don't know if I can," she said. "I'm not used to choosing. I was brought up to believe the men did the choosing."

"That's why men so often find exactly what they want in a woman," I told her. "They know what they like, and they do the choosing."

The Cinderella Syndrome

Even though she was a feminist and a liberated career woman with a busy law practice, Carol found it hard to give up the fantasy of being chosen. In her practice, she fought like a tiger for her clients. In her personal life, she was a wimp, always acted on instead of being the active one. The Cinderella story of meeting the prince by accident at the ball was deeply ingrained in her.

"I don't have any idea how to choose a man," she said. "What if I pick wrong? I don't even know how to flirt in a bar. I just sit there and see who comes over to me. I've never, ever consciously tried to get a particular man. How do you do it?"

Choosing

We started at the beginning, as you should too. We made a list of what Carol wanted in a man. Here's Carol's list.

WHAT I MUST HAVE IN A HUSBAND

Honesty
Trustworthiness
Gentleness
Dependability
Generosity
Sensitivity
Stability

Next, we made another list of what Carol absolutely did not want in a man.

THINGS THAT I CAN'T STAND

Smoking
Drugs
Lying
Workaholics
Cheapskates

Next, we evaluated the last three men Carol had dated. For each man we made a list of his assets and his liabilities. Carol was surprised that each of them had a quality that appeared on her hate list. Armed with her two lists, Carol quickly realized that none of the last three men she had dated qualified as husband material.

Your Criteria versus His Assets and Liabilities

You can qualify men quickly and easily with your own love/hate list. There's one for you to fill in at the back of this book. Start it now, and add to it as further chapters in the book help clarify what's important to you.

You can also qualify a man by making a list of his "assets" (what's positive about him as a future mate) and his "liabilities" (or negative aspects).

As a rule of thumb, a man's assets must include at least eighty percent of your "must have's" or you should drop him. If a man has even one of the qualities you absolutely hate, go on to another one. And if his liabilities greatly outweigh his assets, move on to another man regardless. Even if the man is good company. Even if he's great in bed. You no longer have time to waste on men who tilt your marriage odds in the wrong direction.

Don't worry about your choices being so limited that you just won't be able to bring yourself to drop men who don't qualify. While you're sitting at home or talking with your girlfriends wondering where all the men are, other women are sitting around choosing from hundreds of eligible men, tossing some aside, saving others to consider again, finding a couple of knockouts. Sounds impossible? Don't worry. I'll show you how you can be one of these women.

The first step is to get beyond the Cinderella syndrome and resolve to make choices in your life. Real choices—not just saying yes or no to whomever chooses you. Think about qualifying men for marriage.

To get you started choosing, here are some common-sense criteria that many women ignore:

Recognizing Marriage Material

A man is marriage material if you choose him because he meets your requirements. A man is not marriage material if he chooses you and doesn't fit your requirements.

A man is marriage material if he has been married before and wants to try again. A man is not marriage material if he's still bitter from a divorce.

A man is marriage material if he likes women. A man is not marriage material if he hates his mother, sister, or all lady lawyers.

A man is marriage material if you fill his fantasies. A man is not marriage material if his fantasy woman is totally different from you.

A man is marriage material if he's really ready to get married. A man is not marriage material if he wants to make a million, sail around the world, "find himself" in India, or be a star first.

A man is marriage material if he is sane. A man is not marriage material if he's crazy or acts crazy for whatever reason (including passion).

A man is marriage material if you can trust him. A man is not marriage material if he lies, cheats or is undependable.

It's Okay to Be Particular

Many older single women complicate the task of finding a mate by failing to accept how particular their needs have become. The older you are, the fussier you become. You develop more taste. You're more discriminating, so your choices are more limited. On the other hand, the job of finding the right man among millions of available men becomes much easier because of your well-developed preferences. You'll be more focused in looking and more definite in deciding.

While you can't be unrealistic and expect perfection in a man (see "Compromises and Trade-Offs," Chapter Thirteen), you deserve to have your personal needs met—even if they're too subjective to list in your "must have's." So if a man acts in a way that seems inappropriate *to you*, just drop him and move on. You don't have to justify yourself to anyone. You're not being judgmental, you're being selective.

Janice, a thirty-three-year-old data processing manager, was very taken with Walter when he showed up to install some new software at her office. "Our first date was so much fun," she related. "I loved his sense of humor. We went to a cute movie, and later, at a little jazz club, we found that we both had the same favorites. We talked a lot, and I found he's helping his youngest sister through college.

"He seemed so sweet I didn't hesitate to accept an invitation for dinner at his apartment." Then Janice's face darkened. "Well, I can't begin to describe the place. Really weird science fiction posters and stuff all over, and Walter—he'd forgotten to comb his hair, his shirt had a big stain in front and was hanging out the back and, can you believe, his socks didn't match! I mean, this guy's beyond computer nerd, he's Twilight Zone!"

Pamela had a similar complaint, for a different reason. She was crazy for an attractive bachelor, a Beverly Hills dentist with a big home filled with antiques from his travels. She reported, "I didn't care about Mitchell's fancy house so much, but the sex was great and I thought he really liked me. When he said he was planning a trip to the Far East and would love to take me except that taxes had just wiped him out, I offered to pay my own way. I guess I wanted him to know that I make a good salary, and I wasn't interested in his money.

"But then, when we got away, I couldn't believe it," she continued. "He kept track of all expenses, everything—the tiniest tips—and divided them equally. He had his little calculator with him, and we settled up on the flight back. Then, after I'd written him a check on the plane, he wanted me to pay my share of the airport parking after we left the lot!"

Janice dropped Walter, the "computer nerd," and Pamela saw Mitchell, the dentist, again only a couple of times before ending the relationship. They were both right to do so. If a man has quirks that bother you, they won't go away. They'll just get more pronounced with time.

The funny thing is, if the pairing had been the other way around,

Pamela might have loved Walter for his sweetness, generosity, and science fiction art and not cared at all about his sloppy clothes. Janice might have believed that "a deal's a deal" and viewed Mitchell's fastidious accounting as treating her like an equal.

For both Pamela and Janice, their experiences with these men served to sharpen their focus on what they each need in a man. Janice added "neatness" to her "must have" list, and Pamela added "generosity" to hers.

Three Steps to Success

There are just three steps to marrying later and marrying smarter.

1. You must be the one to choose, to make sure you're only dating men who are truly marriageable and who meet your criteria.

2. You must arrange access to a large number of these men.

3. From this prequalified pool of men, you must only spend time with those who are strongly attracted to you, for whom you are "their type."

By following these common-sense steps, your odds for success will leap past all those other women who are just randomly dating, waiting for someone to choose them. I'll help you through these steps and then provide hints and insights about getting a man to commit and meshing your lives together as a married couple.

But first we'll take a quick look at what may be holding you back, and what you may be doing wrong, to make sure that you avoid other "patterns of failure" that keep women single.

CHAPTER TWO

Why You're Not Married

Sure there's a man shortage, especially if you're over thirty. Yet many women marry. Women all around you marry. Cousins, friends, aged aunts. Women who aren't as smart or pretty or accomplished as you. So why aren't you married?

"I Don't Want a Marriage Like My Parents'"

You are still reacting to your childhood. You don't want a marriage like your parents' marriage, so you avoid any marriage.

To you, marriage means the man's the boss and you have to do what he says. To you, marriage means you will lose your independence, your freedom to party, your selfhood, so you put off being serious about getting married. Then you complain because you haven't had a chance to lose the independence you're protecting.

The truth is, you can't have total independence in marriage. But with the right man, you'll get back far more than you give up.

"Nobody Turns Me On Like Shithead"

You're hooked. You know he's no good for you. But you keep going back. Your friends tell you to get rid of him, and you don't like yourself for being hooked on him, yet you can't stop. He's sleeping with at least one other woman that you know of, plus God knows how many others you don't know about. He sees you just often enough to keep you on his string, but it's not a real relationship. He never says he loves you, and he may even make a point of telling you you're not the woman he wants. He's hurtful, even mean, and you can't stay away from him.

Because of him, you reject nice guys, and a man who loves you back is a big yawn because you're not insecure, scared, being abused or threatened with being left. Your self-esteem is suffering, and you wonder why you put up with "Shithead." Actually, you know why. The sex is great, and you're hooked on unrequited, impossible love.

So get the jerk out of your life, and find someone to love who appreciates you.

"My Mother Said No Man Would Ever Marry Me Because . . ."

"I'm too fat, I'm a slob, I have a big mouth, I'd be a lousy mother. . . ."

So why do you believe your mother all the time? What makes you think she knows more than you do? Besides, lucky you, you don't have to marry someone like your mother. You can find a man who likes you, big mouth and all. Or you could even learn to be quiet once in a while.

"I'm Afraid of Repeating My Last Disaster"

You haven't forgiven yourself, your ex, or men in general. You don't want to let yourself fall in love because you're afraid you'll be left. Men sense your ambivalence, and they draw away. So you're left alone anyway. Might as well fall in love.

"Nobody Wants Me—Men Don't Find Me Attractive"

Even the homeliest women find men to love. If you really want a man, you'll either make yourself more desirable to more men or find men who desire the kind of woman you are.

There are men who love tall women, fat women, bossy women and busy women. Find them (see Chapter Eight), and forget about mooning over men who don't think you're terrific.

"I'm Afraid I'll Lose at Love, so I Don't Try"

You've worked hard to be who you are, accomplish what you have and acquire what you've acquired. You don't like to lose, and love seems so chancy. By not taking a risk with love, you never really lose, but you never win either.

Smart older women who beat the odds take calculated, minimized risks.

"I Date a Lot, but It Never Gets Serious"

You use dating as avoidance, a surface activity to avoid the depth and intimacy of a real relationship. By choosing to date men without first qualifying them as to their marriageability, you ensure that you'll remain single. You use problems that crop up in a new relationship as an excuse to move on and find a new man.

You may have a vague fear of losing self, or you may be recently divorced and still embittered or you may be unable to let go of a past love. Try working out problems next time, instead of leaving.

Be sure you're really ready for a committed relationship. Then use your ability to negotiate. Ask for what you want. You may be surprised when he says yes.

"I've Got Plenty of Time—What's the Rush?"

Women, busy with their careers, will put off marriage for years and then suddenly hit the panic button. "Tracy, help! I want to get married and have two kids by the time I'm forty—in six months—can you help me?"

Although I have a reputation for marrying off my clients, I can't perform miracles. Getting married is not the first act in a relationship. You can usually depend on a few months to find a match, a year for falling in love, getting to know each other and deciding to get married, followed by another six months to plan a wedding. This means that if you start today with no prospects, you could conceivably be married in one and a half to two years. And that's with no margin for error.

A woman will often lull herself into inaction by thinking, "I want to have my first child before I'm thirty-five, but I'm only thirty-two, so I still have plenty of time." She may have plenty of time, but only if she's lucky. More likely, she'll wind up pushing further into her biological timeclock and anxiously hustling to get pregnant in the first year of her marriage—which won't give her and her husband much time to enjoy each other alone.

"He Doesn't Excite Me"

Expecting a man to be both stable—someone you can count on—*and* the source of amusement and excitement in your life is unrealistic.

Ellie should have been on cloud nine. She was thirty-two, had a wonderful guy who totally adored her and wanted to marry her —but she was in torment. At first, as I listened to her story, I was struck by her beauty. She looked at me sorrowfully out of huge brown eyes, set off by a gorgeous mane of dark brown hair. "Mike really loves me, more than anyone else ever has, and he keeps asking me to marry him, but I just can't say yes. He's boring. He doesn't excite me."

When it came to excitement, Ellie was an expert. Like many women, Ellie was a "thrill whore." This didn't mean she did anything for money; it meant she fell for wildly unsuitable men because they were exciting, like in the song "Ladies Love Outlaws." In Ellie's case, the man didn't have to be a biker or sing country songs, but he had to be antisocial and living on the edge. Ellie had an almost-fatal fascination with danger.

After graduating with a fine arts degree from a prestigious Eastern college, Ellie found her way into the fast lane quickly when she fell for an older man dealing in art forgeries in New York City. Because of her proper upbringing, she was troubled at first by the dishonesty involved, but it didn't take long before she was hooked on the lifestyle—trips to Europe, expensive drugs and kinky sex.

The forger was caught and sent to prison, and Ellie narrowly escaped indictment on the same charges. "It was scary, but exhilarating," she confided, "I really felt alive!" Her taste for "excitement" led into a series of dangerous relationships, culminating in a marriage to a stock manipulator. They had a penthouse in Manhattan, a summer home in Southampton and a twin-engine airplane, but he was a heavy cocaine user who physically abused her. She finally had the sense to get out, but even then she was torn.

"It was a very suspenseful time," she related to me. "Jerry had been dealing with one of the guys who got arrested right in his Wall Street office, and we didn't know if the trail would lead back to him or not. So Jerry went into hiding, and I was his link to the world. I loved the 007 routine. But then my father heard about the plastic surgery I had to have after Jerry beat me up. Dad offered to buy me a divorce, and I knew it was a good time to escape."

To get as far as possible from her ex, Ellie came to stay with a girlfriend near the beach in Los Angeles, and that's where she met Mike.

Ellie's men before Mike all had one thing in common: They were far too self-destructive and antisocial to be reasonable husband material. But without the excitement an outlaw type brought into her life, Ellie didn't feel as if she could sustain a relationship. Danger, anxiety and the threat of physical abuse were all mixed into her ideas of love. When she was living on the edge with a man who was dangerous, who might beat her up at any moment, she felt an excitement she confused with love. Mike's love was true, but it was honest, safe love, and boring to her—mostly because she had no excitement in her own life.

Ellie was shocked when I told her that if she was bored, it was her fault, not Mike's. Once Ellie began to take responsibility for providing the excitement she craved, she started appreciating Mike for the wonderful life partner he really was. I asked Ellie, a sports enthusiast, if there were any exciting sports she'd like to try.

It turned out that Ellie had a long-standing urge to take up hang gliding. Mike agreed to try it with her, and they both plunged into the sport. The thrill of hanging in a harness, open to the wind, steering a fragile craft far above the ground proved to be just what Ellie needed in her life. At last she found something more exciting than dangerous relationships.

"It's such a rush, I can't explain it," Ellie reported breathlessly the last time I heard from her. "And, the best part is, Mike loves it, too. I'm going to have to lay off for a few months when I get pregnant, but I'll catch up to him! Oh, and I almost forgot—we're engaged. And I don't mind that it's not the world's biggest diamond, either."

Ellie and Mike are happily married, but only because she woke up to her unrealistic expectations about love—expecting a man to provide all the excitement in her life. Other women have expectations that are different, but equally unrealistic.

Failure Pattern 2: Unrealistic Expectations

Unless you shed your own unrealistic expectations, you might do what Ellie almost did—reject a perfectly wonderful man—and regret it for the rest of your life. Here are some of the more common unrealistic expectations:

1. **You expect a man to fix your life.** Actually, a man can reasonably be expected to love you, be affectionate and "be there" for you. If your car is stuck on the Interstate at night, he's supposed to come get you. If you get the flu, he should take care of you. However, he is *not* responsible for curing your neuroses, solving problems you may have at work or keeping you from being bored.

2. **You expect a man to be perfect.** You won't find a perfect man, you will only trade one imperfection for another one.

So if you can live with the imperfection you find in your man, try to do that. Some other guy's problems may prove intolerable.

3. **You expect a man to make all the moves in a relationship.** A man needs feedback. When he makes a move, he expects a reaction. No reaction is often looked at as no interest. React. Do something. Take the initiative. Let him know you're alive.

4. **You expect anxiety with love.** If you've never experienced love without worrying about being left, without worrying about his cheating on you or abusing you, then you may equate feeling in love with feeling upset. You may not feel loved without feeling anxious. Anxiety is *not* a necessary ingredient in love.

5. **You expect the man you love to be smarter and better than you at everything.** There will be some things he'll do better than you, but you may be amazed to find that there are many things you're better at. Love doesn't depend on the other person being better than you at everything. You really can love someone and still be more competent than he at lots of things.

6. **You expect that "If he loves me, he'll know how I feel."** A man can't read your mind even if he does love you. If you expect him to know and understand how you feel without your having to tell him, you're going to have problems. Often the poor guy won't fully understand how you feel even if you *do* tell him. *Not* telling him, then expecting him to know, is absolutely unrealistic.

7. **You expect him to be loving and totally attentive to you—and still remain a little mysterious.** You can't have it both ways. Mysterious and hard to get are fine for courting. For commitment, you want total love.

8. **You expect a man who loves you to change what you don't like and do anything you want him to do.** After all, *you* have

when you've loved a man. The reality is that he *will* change, and if perchance it's the same thing you want him to change or you've tried to change, you're lucky. He won't do everything you want him to do.

9. **You expect the things that irritate you about him to become less irritating as time goes by.** They won't. Whatever irritates you about your man now will just irritate you more as time goes by. Whatever annoying quirks he has will become more pronounced and more annoying. Don't expect them to go away.

10. **You expect the relationship to remain the same as you get closer.** You expect him to continue to be as romantic as he was in the beginning, to continue to court you just the way he did when you were dating. Courting and dating are exciting phases of a relationship, but they are different from being a committed couple.

CHAPTER THREE

Choosing Men
Who Don't Want You

"I drive home from a wedding, and I'm thinking, 'Why not me? Will it ever be me? Am I going to spend the rest of my life alone?' And then I think, 'Maybe I'm just not lovable.'"

To make Sharon feel better, I began to remind her that most single women get that sad, "always a bridesmaid, never a bride" letdown following a friend's wedding.

"But this is my whole life!" Sharon broke in, "I'm a wedding photographer! When I'm not at a wedding, I'm working on the damn pictures." She began to sob. "I'm thirty-eight years old, I've never been married, and I'm never going to be married.

"I see these brides and grooms, they're so happy, they're so in love, and I die inside. The more my business grows, the worse I feel."

Tears ran down her face. "Can you help me? Please. I'll do anything you say. I just want a man to love me. I'm so tired of being alone."

I could hardly blame her for crying. I imagined how hard it must be for her. Obviously, being single was not something Sharon could escape from by burying herself in her work, as many other women do. Constantly facing happy couples in wedding after wedding had become emotionally devastating for her.

Still, I was puzzled. Looking at her, I couldn't detect any apparent reason for her lack of success with men. A little overweight but very sensual, no raving beauty but not unattractive, Sharon was no better or worse looking than millions of women who find husbands and live happily ever after.

Finally, as we talked, it became clear that Sharon's problem was just one example of choosing men who don't want you.

Failure Pattern 3: Choosing Men Who Don't Want You

Like all too many single women, Sharon tended to ignore men who were attracted to her, spending all her energy pursuing men who weren't interested in her. Sharon's case was particularly sad because of her preference in men.

"I'm really only turned on by younger guys," Sharon confessed to me.

She kept thinking that if only she could change something about herself, she'd get the man she wanted. So various younger men who came into her life were treated to such delights as Sharon talking baby talk or acting frail and helpless—all in an effort to convince them that she was indeed young.

The younger men she wanted were confused by this older woman who ran her own business and wanted to talk baby talk to them. It hadn't occurred to Sharon that if a younger man wanted a woman who would act like a child, he'd pick a woman who was in fact younger, not older.

Women who try to change their personality to attract a man wind up getting a man who doesn't like who they really are. There are things about yourself that you can change and others you can't. After a certain age, your basic personality traits are set. You can change your outward behavior—with a lot of effort—but it's almost impossible to change who you are inside. If you're a good person, you stay a good person. Sharon had to learn to trust that the good person inside her would find a mate. Instead of trying to choose from men who didn't want her, she had to learn to choose from those who did. At first, she had trouble doing this.

When Sharon was around older men, her anxiety to be attractive vanished, and she reverted to the normal-acting, relaxed, competent person she was in business. Older men loved her liveliness, her lack of pretense, her off-the-wall sense of humor, but they turned her off. "He reminds me of my father," she'd say about a man only forty-six. "How could I be serious about someone who reminds me of my father?"

Each session with Sharon seemed to be a replay of the last, filled with her fantasies of how well her meeting with some new younger man went. "But he said he had a great time," she complained. "Doesn't that mean he wants to see me again?"

As a basically up-front person, Sharon couldn't understand that even if a man says he wants to see you again, you can't believe it unless he calls you and asks you out. Men say things to get away, to avoid hurting feelings or having to explain.

Each attractive younger man who paid the least attention to her was a cue for Sharon to start a whole new fantasy. Before she had a chance to go out with a man the second time, sometimes when they hadn't dated at all, she'd begin to fantasize.

And when she hired twenty-six-year-old Rick to help her in her photography studio, she immediately began to fantasize about marrying him. "We get along so well together," she told me. "We laugh all the time. We spend lots of time together, but he never makes a pass at me. I think he likes me but he's just shy."

When Rick moved in with a twenty-two-year-old girl, Sharon was devastated. "We're really right for each other. I know it. Can't he see that?" For months she continued to wallow in her unrequited love for Rick, spending long nights crying on the phone to whomever would listen. She compared each new man she met to Rick. Naturally, none was as much fun, or else they didn't share her enthusiasm for her new photography studio like Rick.

Then Rick broke up with his girlfriend, and Sharon's obsessive thoughts of marrying Rick got worse.

"I'd give him half the business," she told me. "We'd be great together. Besides, we're from the same home town. We're both from Baltimore. Our parents know each other. It's a perfect match." Unfortunately, in Sharon's confused state, she couldn't tell a "perfect match" from an ordinary coincidence.

Avoiding Commitment

Sharon had found a sure-fire way to avoid commitment. What she said turned her on was exactly what kept her from getting what she wanted. She was only excited by what she couldn't have. The instant there was a man she *could* have, she found reasons to dislike him. Sharon set herself up to fail.

If you're a woman who has been choosing only from among men who don't want you, you know who you are. It's time to begin looking into the subtle motives that make you set yourself up to fail at finding a man.

In my seminars I do an exercise where I ask everyone to close their eyes and relax. Then I ask them to imagine that they are at their own wedding, a visualization exercise similar to those used by top athletes to get ready for sporting events. The athletes visualize themselves jumping hurdles, crossing the finish line first—they even hear the cheers. We do the same with our weddings. "Picture yourself getting married. Imagine that today's your wedding day," I tell the participants.

At this point, there are always people who find the exercise difficult. They start to giggle, squirm or wisecrack. As the exercise proceeds, I say, "See yourself on your wedding day. Picture the place where you'll get married. Hear the music playing, 'Here comes the bride, Here comes the bride.' Women, see your dresses, hear the rustle of the tulle and cameras clicking. Look around at your bridesmaids, picture your bridegroom.

"Men, picture your tuxedo, your boutonniere, your best man, your bride. Everyone, take a deep breath, smell the flowers and see your friends and relatives who have come to your wedding. Feel the feelings, the excitement, the nervousness, the love. Hear the words, 'Do you take this woman . . . ? Do you take this man . . . ? Till death do you part. . . .' See yourself exchanging rings. See the ring on your finger. Kiss the bride. Kiss the groom. Hear the wedding march. See your friends gathering around."

Before the exercise is over, some people break into uncontrollable laughter. Some cry. Some refuse to participate because the thought of really getting married is frightening to them.

It's easy to say, "I want to be married. I want to be loved. I want to be in love." But if you can't see yourself getting married, walking down the aisle, or hear yourself reciting vows, you're probably not ready to do it.

Try the exercise yourself. Imagine you're at your own wedding. See yourself in your gown. Picture your bridesmaids, your best man, your parents, friends, minister or rabbi. See the setting, taste the cake, imagine throwing the bouquet. Seeing yourself doing it is the first step toward getting married.

People like Sharon, who have only been involved in the fantasy of having a boyfriend but never the reality of having a solid relationship, are those who have the most trouble imagining themselves at their own wedding. When pressed, Sharon admitted she wasn't sure she really wanted to be married.

"I'm afraid," she confessed. "What if it doesn't work out? What if I get a divorce and wind up like everybody else? What if I'm not happy? What if I have an unhappy marriage?" The real reason for her choice of inappropriate men was emerging—fear of a bad marriage, which was keeping her from any marriage at all.

What finally opened Sharon's eyes was when she hit bottom over having someone to kiss on New Year's Eve.

"I don't have a boyfriend," Sharon cried hysterically. "It's going to be New Year's Eve, and I don't have a date. What's wrong with me?"

So she finagled an invitation to join Rick and another friend, Julian, for a New Year's Eve concert. Then Rick, to avoid being stuck with Sharon, bought a fourth ticket and invited an old girlfriend. Sharon was in tears again. "I know Julian likes me, but he doesn't turn me on. I want Rick."

After the disastrous event, Sharon related, "We'd all had a few drinks, and I told Rick it would solve all his problems if he just fell in love with me." I wished I'd been able to put the words back in Sharon's mouth.

"And I told him the most important thing to me was having someone to kiss on New Year's at the stroke of midnight." It was hard to believe that Sharon would set herself up once again to be hurt by Rick. Needless to say, he disappeared when the clock struck midnight.

"There I was standing all by myself while everyone around me was kissing someone. It was horrible," she cried. "I'd have been better off staying home alone."

I was shocked and saddened by how badly Rick had treated Sharon, and Sharon was a wreck. Just as a friend and coworker, Rick could have given Sharon a little mercy kiss and a hug. Big deal. "He knew it was important to me, and he just left me standing there. How could he?"

In spite of how bad she felt, Sharon found it impossible to stand up to Rick and tell him how she felt.

"What would happen if you told him you were angry with him for leaving you alone at midnight on New Year's?" I asked her. "I'm afraid," she answered.

"Afraid of what?" I asked her.

"That he'll leave me?" Sharon looked up and managed a small laugh. Even she had to realize that she didn't *have* Rick, so how could he leave her?

Fear of Failure

Sharon's New Year's Eve humiliation was a turning point for her. She realized she was afraid of failing so she wasn't really trying to find an appropriate man. The result was that she remained single and unhappy. "I guess I might as well take a chance on being married and happy," she told me.

At last, Sharon was ready. I made out a game plan for her, so that she could realize her goal of being married by the time she was forty. She followed my man-finding suggestions and succeeded in meeting a wide variety of new men. Most important, she learned the wisdom of choosing from among men who are ready to settle down and who are attracted to her, rather than fantasizing about young men who weren't giving her a second glance.

Breaking the Failure Pattern

Once Sharon replaced her failure patterns with success patterns, her dating life became a source of fulfillment instead of frustration. In less than three months she started seeing one man quite steadily. After Valentine's Day, she reported, "I just had the best Valentine's Day of my whole life. Alan is everything I want in a man. He says all the right words and does all the right things. He sent me a card, bought me flowers and took me out. I can't believe I ever made such a fool of myself over Rick."

When I last spoke to her, she and Alan were about to leave on a trip to Mexico. She sounded like a different person. She began to adjust her schedule to allow for some weekends off. She and Alan are currently talking about moving in together and are planning a trip to Baltimore to meet her parents.

"I have a real boyfriend. We're going on a trip. I've never been on a trip with a man before. I've never been this happy."

You're probably wondering, what was the plan she followed? Was it that easy? No, but after years of relationship failures, Sharon found success surprisingly fast. We'll pick up her story—exactly how she found Alan—in Chapter Eight.

Like Sharon, you can change your life by starting to choose from among the men who really want to be with you and discarding those who don't.

CHAPTER FOUR

Special Problems of Smart, Successful Women

Women Who Scare Men Away

We've seen it happen over and over again. High-achieving, high-energy, high-earning women scare men off. What exactly scares these men? Deeply rooted, almost unconscious fears of being hurt or dominated.

Among young men, raw strength determines the pecking order. Having learned to fear physical power, men react the same way to women who are intellectually, emotionally and financially powerful. They back off.

A woman who is more powerful in the areas of career and money often has to go to some lengths to prove that she can be vulnerable, that she actually needs a man and that she can be happy in a non-autonomous situation.

Rachel, dressed in a designer suit, tapped her Feragamo shoes impatiently. "The point is that I want a man. My life is perfect except for the one missing ingredient, a man to share it with. Just tell me what to do, and I'll do it."

Rachel's offices in downtown L.A. were only two blocks from

her high-rise penthouse condomimium. She walked to work at seven in the morning, worked until eight or nine at night and then walked home.

"What's your fantasy of how your life with a man would be different?" I asked her.

"Well, he could come by the office and walk me home at night. I'd have someone to escort me to functions. I'd be loved, and I wouldn't have to feel inadequate about not having a man in my life. I'd have someone to play golf with in foursomes at the country club. We'd travel a lot, and I'd feel complete. I've been in large groups of women lately and I'm the only one who's never been married. I'm thirty-seven and it's time."

Amazingly, Rachel's fantasy about her life with a man included nothing she would do in his life, only how he'd fit into hers.

"Men say I intimidate them. It's because I'm smarter than most men. I make more money than most men, too. I wouldn't mind a man who doesn't make quite as much as I do, but he'd have to be a white-collar, creative person. I'd really prefer a man who earns more, though."

Rachel's past love life had been sporadic. In between brief affairs with executives like herself, she would find time for occasional recreational sex with someone who seemed undemanding and attractive. She had never been engaged, lived with anyone or come close to marriage. Now she was ready to make getting married a priority in her life.

The first thing she had to do was stop scaring men.

"It's not me, it's them," she insisted. "They're just not good enough, and they know it. That's why they're intimidated by me. But if they would just give me a chance, they'd see that I can be warm and affectionate and very sexy once I get to know a man." She paused, uncomfortable with talking about her emotions, and then added, "I just never get a chance to show off that side of myself. I'm so busy pushing and shoving to get ahead, I sometimes lose touch with the other me."

From "I" to "We"

The first step for Rachel was to learn how to use the words, "you" and "we" instead of "I" and "me." She was so used to thinking in terms of just herself in her life that she had become totally self-centered. Simply changing the pronouns she used when she was with men gave a less self-centered aspect to her communication, but she would have to change even more before she found the man of her dreams.

Changing the way she thought about men was the next step. Instead of seeing men as objects to be acquired, she had to begin thinking of men as partners in life.

"When you meet the next new man you like," I told her, "I want you to treat him just as you would if you were taking in a new partner in your business. You'd want to make that new partner feel comfortable. You'd want to draw him out and get his ideas. You'd want to make him feel like he's part of your team."

Being part of a business team was easy for Rachel, but she had never before thought about a personal relationship with a man as being a team effort. The whole concept was new to her. It meant that instead of competing with a man, she would work with him. Instead of having a push-pull power struggle, it could be the two of them pulling together.

One big problem Rachel had was that she'd become so independent as a single. She was used to doing exactly what she wanted to do, how and when she wanted to do it. Rachel didn't realize that she would have to give up some of her autonomy to have a good relationship.

Who Gets to Be Boss

Instead of being the boss all the time, I pointed out to her that she'd have to accept being the boss about a fourth of the time. "Wait a minute!" she interrupted, going right into her negotiating mode. "Why should the man get to be boss three-quarters of the time? Whose side are you on, anyway?"

Rachel's lack of relationship experience made her think decisions would be split fifty-fifty—at worst, she would have added. "The way an equal life partnership works out in the real world," I explained to her, "is that the man also gets to be the boss about a fourth of the time, and the rest of the time nobody is boss because you both wind up compromising."

Who gets to be boss is often an issue when you marry later. You're each used to being in charge, to being totally autonomous, to having your own way.

When you're single, you don't have to compromise. But if you want to be in a committed relationship, you just can't be the boss all the time. You can't control someone else's behavior, so you have to give up being boss to live with another person.

For Rachel, who was an only child and who'd always been encouraged to be independent and to make her own decisions, giving up being boss was the hardest part of having a relationship.

Making Room for a Man

When I visited Rachel's apartment for a cocktail party she was giving, I could see how a man would have trouble seeing himself in Rachel's surroundings. The bathroom, for example, was so filled with her makeup and perfumes and various preparations that a man wouldn't have been able to find space for his toothbrush, let alone a can of shaving cream.

In the bedroom, Rachel had created a feminine fantasy of lace and pillows and more frilly, fussy pinks and pastels than I had ever seen before. Any male would definitely have felt out of place in her surroundings.

The furniture in the living room was Queen Anne style, lovely antiques, but not exactly the kind of "sink in, feel good, put your feet up" kind of surroundings men yearn for. Her china was so delicate and precious that a man would have had trouble holding a coffee cup.

There was also no evidence of Rachel's nurturing ability anywhere in the apartment. No family photos to show that she loved her mother, father, or other relatives. No plants to be watered, no pets to be fed.

Rachel had to learn to let a man see that she could be a nurturing person. Rachel's kind of man wouldn't want her to be Betty Crocker, but he would expect to see a picture of her being loving and supportive in some way or another. Even better, if he could see her feeding a pet, giving the kind of unconditional love we tend to give to our animals, it would suggest that he could get that kind of affection from her too. Otherwise, how would he ever suspect that inside this hard-boiled businesswoman beats the heart of a mommy, a wife, a life partner?

Rachel immediately caught on. She bought some houseplants, got rid of the tangle of lace on her bed, got a comfortable leather couch that a man could actually stretch out on and even went pet shopping.

She fell in love with a kitten, then the kitten's sister, then the kitten's brother. All of a sudden she had three little kittens chasing through her apartment. From that day on her life changed. A man could see instantly that she wasn't always in control—in her home, the cats were—and that she loved them in spite of the havoc they wrought, scratching the furniture, climbing up her designer suits and knocking things off shelves. Being in her life began to look like fun.

Best of all, the nurturing part of her personality blossomed, and she felt better about herself. "Even if all this doesn't attract a man, it's great for my stress level," she wisecracked.

Within a year, Rachel met Jonas, a top executive for a large corporation, while she was doing volunteer work on the Los Angeles Olympic Committee. He was everything she wanted. He even played golf. Soon they were engaged. A little of the old Rachel remained, though. "My fiancé doesn't always do what I want him to do," she complained. I assured her that my husband doesn't always do what I want him to do, either.

Her wedding was the media event of the season. But even after she was married, Rachel had to fight her desire to be the boss.

Going Into Business Together

Sharon, the wedding photographer whose foolish pursuit of a younger man was described in Chapter Three, made a further relationship error by getting that young man involved in her business.

No matter how often I counsel women against this, they keep doing it. The fantasy of working together to build a little empire is out of control in women business owners. Actually, according to many interviews I've conducted with women who've been in business and in love with the same man, the success of the business almost always means the failure of the relationship. And if the business fails, the relationship suffers, too. You can't win.

Many years ago I got involved in writing a book with a man I was having a relationship with. It turned out to be one of the worst experiences of my life. Two strong egos with our own ideas about running a project, we constantly clashed. Two people who were used to having control suddenly had to give up some. The relationship shattered in a series of stormy fights, but that wasn't the end of it. We couldn't just break up and get away from each other because we were partners in the book, which stayed in print for years after, creating ongoing opportunities for disagreement over resale rights, updated cover material and anything else requiring our mutual consent.

I'm sure one of the reasons I was able to marry my husband was that in spite of the temptation, I refused to become involved in business dealings with him. I can remember, soon after we met, when he wanted his production company to option some motion picture scripts I had written. My best friend said, "Good. But just do business with him. Why have a relationship? You'll only mess things up."

Fortunately, I opted for the relationship rather than the business deal, but I knew my friend was right about not having it both ways, so I didn't try. You can't have the perfect business partner and the perfect mate too. Usually when men and women work together, the man makes all the power moves and the woman does all the administrative work—typing contracts and proposals, photocopying, going to the post office, buying office supplies, not to mention making coffee and cleaning up. The man's work is creative and fun—"taking meetings," "doing lunch," and making deals. Naturally you resent him for taking all the excitement away from you.

If *you* insist on conducting the meetings, lunches and negotiations, the man in your life will naturally resent you for taking that part away from him. So if you want to be the boss, don't make the man in your life your employee. You'll be creating an impossible situation.

Even going into an equal partnership with the man you love can be extremely dangerous to your relationship—no matter how tempting it seems.

Elaine made Mike a partner in her film business. She had been making educational films, but she had great ideas for general interest films. She could become Steven Spielberg, she dreamed, if only she had the financing. Mike seemed to be the answer to her dreams.

They met on the slopes at Aspen. Mike, a former investment banker, had dropped out and was living the life of an upscale ski bum, supporting himself with the money he'd made from a large deal that went public. They fell in love, and Elaine began to see her dreams come true as she convinced Mike to raise money for one of her film projects.

Mike, unable to resist the temptation to build another empire, stepped into Elaine's business, giving up his life at Aspen and moving with her to Los Angeles.

He succeeded in raising the money, but it soon became clear that they had different ideas about what kinds of films to make. Mike wanted to make commercial movies, action movies filled with killings and chases. The ethereal Elaine wanted to make artsy spiritual films filled with messages of good will. Mike insisted they had a responsibility to their investors to recoup their investments, and he and Elaine fought constantly. It didn't take long for the two of them to break up both the business and their relationship. They lost the condo in Aspen and the love they had for each other.

Elaine went back to making educational films, and Mike made a few B movies before deciding to go back into the investment banking business. Elaine and Mike might still have been together, skiing at Aspen and enjoying each other's company if they hadn't become business partners. So the best advice is don't, no matter how tempted you are, use business as a way to entice a man. Whether the business succeeds or fails doesn't matter, you'll ruin the relationship.

Being in business together just gives you one more thing to fight about. It permeates your life. You bring it home with you, and you continue to argue over it into the evening and sometimes even in bed. If business is good, you're too busy to have time for each other. If business is bad, you're too depressed and too broke to have any fun.

Financially, you're better off as a couple if you're in different businesses entirely. That way if one of you has a bad year, the other one can carry you both. If you're in business together, a bad year can be devastating—financially and emotionally. You won't be able to keep from wondering whose fault it is.

CHAPTER FIVE

Improving Your Personal Odds

If this is your time to find a husband, it's also time to get your act together. You'll enhance your personal odds of marrying by putting your best foot forward.

Do you present yourself in the most flattering light, or could you do something to improve your appearance? Do you "connect" well with men, or are you always saying to yourself, "If only he knew the 'real me,' I know he'd like me?" Many women avidly attend "dress for success" classes and "business communication" seminars but then are insulted if anyone suggests that they could improve the ways in which they relate to men.

Failure Pattern 4: Refusal to Make Changes

Now I can just hear lots of you saying, "Why should I have to change myself to get a man?" The answer is that you don't have to change at all. There's probably a man out there somewhere who would love you in your rattiest jeans and grumpiest mood, but the inescapable fact is that how you dress and how you handle yourself with men affects how they respond to you.

Let's be realistic. Do you know any woman who doesn't get all gussied up for an exciting first date? Do you know a single woman who doesn't act just a little differently when she's in a group of men? Of course not. The question is not *whether* you're going to dress and act differently when interacting with men; the question is *how*. Sometimes it's hard for a woman to know whether the way she's presenting herself is helping or hurting her. It's amazing how many women are shooting themselves in the foot by doing exactly the wrong things.

Finding out what you may be doing wrong with men can be painful, and it's also difficult, because you can't rely on men to tell you. On the rare occasions when a man does tell the truth, you probably won't believe him. We women always think there's more to why a man doesn't want us than he says.

Image Tune-Ups: Looks, Personality, Sexual Attitude

Men respond to women in a multitude of ways, but the primary categories, not surprisingly, are (1) looks, (2) personality, and (3) sexual rapport. Looks are probably the easiest to work with. Personality is a lot harder to change. Sexual rapport can be improved if a man is responding to your looks and personality.

Starting with the category of looks, you can use a simple feedback technique to find out if there's anything you need to change. Common sense and your budget will tell you what's changeable, and then you alone can decide what you're willing to change.

Ask someone you trust for feedback, using the wording suggested below. You'll be surprised at how a specific request for help will get you information you've always wanted but have never known how to get before. Remember, this exercise is not about what's wrong with you, it's about what men might want and what you can and can't do differently. While you're getting the feedback, don't argue. Don't comment. Just say, "Yes, and what else is there?"

Looks

Feedback about looks should start out, "If I were a man who was thinking about having a relationship with you, I could be worried about your looks if . . ."

"I wanted a tall woman."

"I wanted a woman with long hair."

"I wanted a woman who was slim."

"I wanted a woman who dressed elegantly."

Don't expect all feedback to be a total revelation—just think about it. The preceding examples were given to Cynthia, age thirty-three, by a friend.

"So some men don't think I'm tall enough," she told me. "Well, that's obvious. I've known that all my life, and there's nothing I can do about it.

"I sure don't enjoy a reminder that I could be slimmer. That's obvious, too, but it *is* something I could change. . . .

"And there are some things I haven't thought about recently— my hair, for example. You know, I used to get lots of compliments when I was wearing it long. Maybe I should let it grow out.

"But the 'dressing elegantly' really surprises me. What's that all about? No one's ever told me that. I thought I dressed just fine. Maybe I should get some advice on how to dress more elegantly."

I told Cynthia that she was responding well to the feedback, and that what she decided to act on was totally up to her.

Actually, your appearance is the easiest thing about yourself to change. This feedback process will give you some ideas on how to look your best. Consider what you're willing to change; then, once you're satisfied you've done what you can, quit worrying about looks.

Don't be intimidated if you're just average-looking and you meet a terrific-looking man who's always been with beauty queens. A man who's been around has learned that life is not a beauty contest. Remember, if the beauty queens were so great, he wouldn't be unattached.

As one extremely attractive man said, "I've had my *Playboy* centerfold, now I want a real woman." For many men, an experience with a beautiful "airhead" is just what they need to make them appreciate someone just like you.

Personality

Feedback about your personality should start out, "If I were a man who was thinking about having a relationship with you, I could be worried about your personality if . . ."
"I wanted a woman who would let me be boss."
"I wanted a woman who would stay home with the kids."
"I wanted a woman who was a gourmet cook."
"I wanted a woman who would move to different cities."
If you're a woman getting this feedback, it should be clear that lots of men will be put off by your independence and your commitment to your career. But they may be attracted by your looks and take five dates to realize that you're not for them. So the idea here is not for you to change your personality but to fine-tune your awareness. The faster your radar can detect a guy who wants a traditional homemaker, the less time you'll waste on personality mismatches. Check your criteria for choosing a man—is "liberated" or something similar on your "must have" list to remind you?

Sexual Attitude

Feedback about your sexual personality should start out, "If I were a man who was thinking about having a relationship with you, I could be worried about your sexual attitude if . . ."
"I wanted a woman who touched a lot."
"I wanted a woman who wore sexy clothes."
"I wanted a woman who was sexually sophisticated."
"I wanted a woman who thought sex was fun."
If you were the woman getting this kind of feedback, you'd have to accept the notion that you don't make a sexy impression. If being sexy isn't a priority in your life, that's fine; keep doing what you're doing and you'll probably find a like-minded man.

If, however, this impression is misleading—if you do feel that you're a sensual woman—then you've gotten your clue to project it more. You could learn to become more sexually aware.

Watch sexy women. They're physically flirtatious. They touch their bodies a lot; they cross and uncross their legs. They pout their lips. They blink their eyes and toss their hair. They touch men easily and comfortably. They radiate that they really like men and that they like being touched. While affection is not the same as sex, you should be aware that an "affectionate" woman is another prime male requirement.

In all these feedback exercises, be careful not to ask just anybody to help, or you could wind up acting pretty silly.

Patty, a petite blonde with a traffic-stopping figure and a great face to go with it, sat in my office one day and cried because she asked the wrong person what was keeping men away from her. He told her, "All men want a Florence Nightingale type. You're too sexy. You intimidate men with your sexuality."

Instead of realizing that this man was telling her she was too sexy for *him* and that *he* wanted a Florence Nightingale type, Patty tried to act like a virgin/Florence Nightingale on her next several dates. Naturally, each man thought she was acting strangely. Here was this exceptionally sexy woman trying to act like Mary Poppins.

If you want reliable feedback, always ask someone who knows you well and whom you can trust to be objective—another woman or a man with whom you have no involvement.

But you might need more. You might need feedback from a pro. Dating is a skill. You may have developed some bad dating habits, just as bad habits can creep into someone's tennis or golf game. Smart players periodically take a lesson from a pro to detect and correct those bad habits. If you're having serious problems getting second dates with the men you want, maybe you need some professional "date coaching."

"Date Coaches"

When Diane, a successful television producer, came to me for help, I was almost afraid I'd met my match. She was about forty pounds overweight, too heavy for most men, but not heavy enough to turn on the guys who like "jiggle." Her bleached blonde hair was a mess, and her denim and silver suede outfit made her look even larger. "I hear you get women married," she told me, adding in typical Hollywood style, "I understand if somebody just knows you, they get married, just from hanging around you for a while. So what can you do for me?"

I told her that to be competitive and get a man in the Hollywood arena, she'd have to lose weight and make herself more attractive. "Yeah, I know. I'm dieting. And I'm a chinless wonder, but I already have an appointment with the plastic surgeon."

She lost weight, got a chin, shaped up, and began making dates. But after going out with fourteen different men who didn't call back after the first meeting, she was totally distraught. "What's wrong with me?" she wailed, tears streaking the mascara down her cheeks. "Why don't I have a boyfriend? Why doesn't anyone want to see me again? Am I such a dog?"

Actually, with her new chin and her weight loss, Diane wasn't a dog at all. She was quite attractive. "I must be doing something wrong. I wish I could take you on a date with me and you could sit in the corner and listen and tell me what I'm doing wrong."

Naturally, I couldn't go on a date with Diane, but I asked her what happened on her dates.

"I've tried so many things," she said. "I've tried to be peppy and make bright conversation. And sometimes I've acted dumb, sitting and smiling and not saying a word all night. I've let them talk, and I've tried to be a good listener. It just ain't working."

Knowing how well-educated men look for "class" in a woman and how quickly they can be put off by speech patterns that aren't feminine, I gently asked Diane why she said "ain't" instead of "isn't."

"It's just the way I talk, I guess," she said.

Diane didn't know why she used the kind of street grammar and slang she did. After all, she'd been to college. She knew better. "I guess I tried to be a guy for my dad and that's the way I talk to impress men."

That approach is fine if you want to be one of the guys at the Saturday softball game. But not for romance.

Diane definitely needed a "date coach" to go along on a date with her. The question was, How? Then I had an idea: The next time Diane went out, she left a tape recorder running in her purse. When we listened to it together later, she was astounded.

In addition to her odd use of slang, Diane had spent the whole date trying to impress the man with how much she owned. She had managed to talk about her new condo, her new car, her expensive stereo, her big-screen television and big business scores, as well as dropping what seemed to be every name in Hollywood. And almost every sentence she said started with the word "I."

"I guess I sound like I'm bragging," she said.

Actually, it was far worse. She sounded desperate, as if she had to impress a man fast or he'd get away. And it was a little insulting to the man too, with the implication that he was only interested in the possessions in her life. Even taking her on a materialistic level, if her life was so complete, what could a man contribute?

The recorder worked very effectively as an inexpensive "date coach" for Diane. She now realized that her bragging was a turnoff, and by talking like an uneducated person, she was alienating educated men and attracting the kind of men she didn't want.

Diane began to understand that she should be herself with men, but her best self. Nevertheless, she still had a way to go. By dressing like a flashy floozy, she was still sending the wrong signals.

Seeing Yourself through Others' Eyes

Since Diane really couldn't see what was wrong with her but was willing to change whatever she was doing wrong, I referred her to a professional media trainer/image consultant who works with politicians and corporate executives on how to present themselves to the public and the press—a different kind of "date coach." I had sent other clients to this trainer in the past, with some simple instructions on what kind of on-camera situation to set up and what kinds of questions to answer. The results were dramatic each time. Seeing themselves played back on the video enabled my clients, for the first time, to see themselves as a man sees them.

"No wonder men leave," said one woman, whose problem was

lack of eye contact. "I'm looking down, or out the window, the whole time!" Janet, a vociferous, outgoing, strong woman suddenly became soft-spoken and shy in a date situation, which she'd never quite realized until she viewed her tape. It was easy to see that a man would be shocked when he later found out who was really behind the shy and breathy voice.

Diane, after several sessions with the media coach, was like a new person. No longer zigzagging between looking schlumpy and flashy, she had developed her own sense of style. Always eager as a puppy, she had never had a problem with positive body language, looking alive and interested and making eye contact; all she had to learn was how to tone down her conversational style to make it more intimate. With her new-found confidence, she no longer felt compelled to brag, and her natural sweetness and charm began to emerge.

In less than a year, Diane's life completely turned around. What she calls me about now is not a lack of men or second dates, but who to select from a surplus of eligible men.

With Jayne, another of my clients, the same combination of tape recorder and media training provided exactly the "date coaching" she needed to identify traits that made her lots of fun but not exactly lovable.

Jayne, age thirty-seven, a buyer for a major department store, was invited to every party. Her loud laughter made a group come alive. Her quick comebacks and funny put-downs made her popular. She had lots of friends, but lovers were few and far between, and they left almost as fast as they appeared.

Like Diane, she was surprised at how she sounded when we reviewed the tape recording after one of her dates. "I'm the one who's always talking—and without thinking first, it seems," she groaned. "My voice is so loud, and my New York accent makes me sound like a put-down comedian, like Don Rickles or Joan Rivers. I can see how a man might not like it. Not only doesn't he get to talk, but he probably worries that he'll be the butt of my jokes when we're with other people." She also heard something else on the tape that she hadn't been aware of.

"I guess I never realized it, but most of my jokes that don't put someone else down put *me* down, especially about my being single. Boy, that's not doing me any good, either."

In sessions with the media trainer, Jayne worked on her overall presentation—her colors, hair, clothes and particularly her voice. When she talked softly, her loud, obnoxious voice became deep and sexy. She worked on not being the first one to talk. On taking time to think before she said anything. On sounding more vulnerable and feminine.

Soon she had a chance to use her new voice on a brand-new man in her life. The last time I heard from her, she was ecstatic.

"It's a miracle. He liked me on the phone, we met and he still likes me. I've never been so happy. We're planning a trip to the Bahamas together. I really think we could get married. He's everything I want."

Candice, age thirty-three, a Beverly Hills divorcée, had a somewhat different problem. As a member of an expensive video dating service, she never had a shortage of dates, but nothing romantic or permanent ever seemed to develop out of them. Her light brown hair was cut short and tipped with blonde. Her figure was absolutely perfect, without an ounce of fat anywhere. Her clothes were well tailored and in excellent taste, obviously expensive. She usually wore Escada or Louis Feraud suits for dates.

Candice's colors were great, her hairstyle and makeup were exquisite, and she had a pleasant speaking voice. But she projected an overly perfect, cool image.

Again, the media trainer was able to point out to Candice how she could be warmer, more approachable. Instead of crisp linens, she should wear soft cashmere sweaters—just as chic, but so much more touchable. She could grow her hair into a more touchable style, without the little spikes that were interesting, but slightly offputting. She could be more vulnerable by letting a man find a thread to pick off her once in a while or by having a wisp of hair out of place.

If, like Diane and Jayne and Candice, you're having a problem with first dates not turning into second ones, get some feedback. Try listening to a recording of how you sound talking to a man on a date. (Afterwards, be sure to erase the tape to maintain the privacy of the conversation—the idea here is to help you, not to make secret recordings of men.)

If feedback from friends indicates that you might be able to improve your overall "presentation," you can probably find a professional image consultant or media trainer if you live near a large city. This kind of coaching is expensive, but it can be very effective. Be prepared to spend $50 to $250 per hour depending on the facilities provided.

Even if you can't afford or don't have access to a professional media trainer, you can get together with a couple of girlfriends, rent a video camera and record how you come across in a dating-type situation. Tape yourself in various outfits to see what looks best. One of your friends can run the camera, and the other can act as your "date," asking you the kinds of questions that will draw you out. Then you can trade places. Here are some of the questions I have my media trainer ask in my "date coaching" process.

Describe your ideal man.
Describe your ideal relationship. The things you'd like to do together.
What are you like when you're in a relationship?
What do you expect of a man who loves you?
How would you describe yourself to a prospective date?
What are your long-range plans for marriage, career, motherhood?
What are the things you absolutely, positively can't stand?
What do you absolutely, positively insist on?

Add your own questions to the list. If you can recruit a guy with whom none of you is involved to play the "date," so much the better.

Practice

As you improve your presentation and hone your dating skills, it's vitally important to practice them, just as you'd practice what the tennis pro told you about correcting your stroke. Use your best dating skills even when you wind up on a date with a man you can tell you're not going to go out with again.

Setting Limits

As a matter of fact, it's easier to practice some dating skills when you're *not* hot for a guy than when you are. For example, starting with every first date, practice setting limits. That is, learn to let a man know that it's not acceptable to be late without calling or to flirt with other women when he's with you. Setting limits shows you're a sane person who acts in your own best interests.

Most women fail to set limits at the beginning of a relationship, which is exactly when it must be done. Some women do it, but too harshly. It takes practice to set limits nicely but firmly, without destroying the romantic mood. Start now to make it one of your basic dating skills, so that when you do fall madly in love with someone, you'll be able to keep him from walking all over you.

Even after you've gotten your act totally together and you're the best that you can be, you'll still be able to find men who don't want you. If you choose men who aren't available or aren't interested in you, you'll be wasting your new-found knowledge. The next chapter will help you spot some types to avoid.

CHAPTER SIX

Men Who Won't Marry You

Getting hung up on men who are unsuitable, unable to make a commitment or both is one of the best ways to stay unmarried.

Failure Pattern 5: Choosing Ineligible Men

My most unsuitable man was a member of a rock 'n' roll band. He had long hair, some interesting tattoos, used every kind of drug imaginable and was great in bed. His life of clubs, touring, all-night recording sessions and endless partying was fun to visit, but I wouldn't want to live there. And I admit, I was addicted to him sexually, which made him hard to leave—but, of course, he was no one I could ever spend the rest of my life with. I could hardly introduce him to my friends, let alone marry him. Whenever one of my group met him, they'd roll their eyes and swear I'd lost my mind.

Not all unsuitable men are so obvious. A women can fall for one and become emotionally dependent before she realizes that the man is unsuitable or unavailable.

Time Wasters

If you're twenty and can't resist a fling with one of the Rogue's Gallery listed below, that's one thing. But if you're over thirty and looking for a marriage partner, *don't waste your time* with one of these. They may appear eligible at first, and they may ultimately live with you and even love you (in their fashion), but they won't marry you. If you're over thirty and are involved with one of these guys, dump him immediately.

Men Who Don't Respond to You

If you date a man and he doesn't respond in normal ways, drop him. He could be gay. He could be neurotic. He could simply not be turned on by you. It really doesn't matter too much why he doesn't respond.

If he doesn't call after a reasonable amount of time, don't wait around. If he isn't reasonably affectionate and interested in sex, drop him. If he doesn't spend romantic time with you, it's because he doesn't want to, and it doesn't matter why.

If he does spend time with you but you don't feel like you're getting love from him, if he just doesn't seem to be a loving person, don't try to analyze him. Don't try to play shrink, just forget about him.

In my seminars I always tell the story of the little boy who went to the circus with his mother. The boy spots a bright red popcorn machine painted with clowns. "Mommy, mommy, there's a popcorn machine. Buy me popcorn. Please, mommy." So the mother gives the boy a quarter to put in the popcorn machine. The boy puts the quarter in the machine and nothing happens. He runs back and gets his mother, and she comes over. Through the glass sides, she can see that the machine is filled with lots of buttery-looking popcorn. She puts another quarter in the machine. It still doesn't work. She pushes it, shakes it and nothing comes out. The little boy starts to cry. "I can see the popcorn, Mommy, why can't we get some?"

"The popcorn machine is broken," says the mother. "There's

nothing we can do. It needs a popcorn machine repairperson to fix it."

Some men are just like the broken popcorn machine. Only with them, the thing that won't come out is love. They look just fine from the outside. You can sense they have love to give. They may even say they want to be in love, but they are not loving. If you have a man who's like the broken popcorn machine, don't keep putting in quarters, wondering what you're doing wrong or how you should change. It's no use, and it's not your fault. He needs the kind of repair work you can't provide. You just have to move on to another man.

Men Who Have Made Great Sacrifices

Years ago I interviewed a beautiful movie star in Aspen, Colorado. She was young, in her prime, glamorous, intelligent—and disgusted with the men in Aspen.

"They're all Ph.D. college professors who've dropped out to live the life of a ski bum. They work way below their intellectual capacity in menial jobs, and the only thing they care about is their skiing.

"Their love for this lifestyle is all-consuming. They sacrifice their education, careers and families for it. They've already given their all. What importance does a woman have in their lives? None.

"Sure, they're willing to hang out with you, but they'll shove you aside in a second if you get in the way. Most of the time the screwing you get isn't worth the screwing you're getting."

So be sure that you can be important in a man's life. Pick a man who is available to adore you, not one who already adores something else more than he'd ever adore a woman.

Men Who Want to Be Stars

Men driven to be stars of some kind are lousy prospects for marriage. They're like workaholics, only worse. Their dreams of stardom totally eclipse any interest in a normal life and a normal marriage. And hidden within those dreams lurks a cruel reality for the woman who helps such a man in his quest: The prize for his success includes *women*—young, beautiful, available women in endless supply.

It has always been so. Whether a man is a showbiz celebrity, a charismatic politician, a military dictator, an investment banking star or just a behind-the-scenes wielder of great wealth and power, women are part of the payoff. The sexual escapades of the rich and powerful are frequent sources of gossip, yet sex is rarely acknowledged as a *reward* for success. But don't kid yourself. Every man who has his sights on the top understands the deal very clearly.

Most women seem to be oblivious to this reality. I'm always amazed at the number of phone calls I get from women who are sure that some celebrity is just the one for them—not just as a fantasy roll in the hay, but as a husband!

Janine was hot for the star of a sitcom. The first thing she did was to change jobs so that she could work in "The Industry" to be closer to him. She collected information and clippings about him in a scrapbook until she knew more about him than his own mother. Then she wrangled a VIP invitation to the shooting of his show. While there, she presented him with a needlepoint pillow she had made with his name and a big star—in his favorite colors, of course. Afterwards, she was delirious.

"He came right over to me," she said. "He got real close, like right between my breasts. He didn't have to get that close," she added, hoping to give weight to her belief that he really cared for her. "He held my hand, he kissed me and I turned my head at just the right moment and his lips touched mine."

After that, she was unstoppable. She wouldn't take my advice to leave it at a kiss, but she did keep coming to see me, reporting on her campaign. Janine was certainly diligent. She volunteered to work for her star's favorite charity, fantasizing about him escorting her to the charity ball. She became editor of the charity's newspaper, which enabled her to interview him for articles. After that, she felt successful whenever he deigned to talk to her. "He knows me by name," she bragged to me. "He's beginning to like me, I can tell. I have a special feeling about this man. I know we're meant to be together. Even if we don't fall in love, I know we'll become good friends." When he went to the charity ball with someone else, Janine was crushed.

Unfortunately, to him she was just another fan who had the good taste to see how wonderful he was. He accepted her gifts, smiled, bussed her Hollywood style, but the relationship never went any further. All Janine did was waste many precious months—time that she could have spent looking for a real, normal, human being–type husband.

Married Men

Some married men will say they're "just a little bit married," that their wives "don't understand them" or that they "haven't had sex with their wives for years," that they and their wives have an "understanding" that they're "just waiting until the kids leave home and they'll get a divorce." Don't believe any of it.

This category of time waster seems almost too obvious to discuss, but women keep coming to me for counseling because they're hung up on a married man. It can happen to anyone.

I'm sure I would have been married sooner if I'd simply avoided all married men. But like many women, I had to learn the hard way. I dated two married men seriously. One was separated when I met him. After a year of dating me, he got his wife (with whom he swore he wasn't sleeping) pregnant.

The other one didn't tell me he was married until we had been dating for several weeks. I was too much in love and too stupid to stop seeing him right away. Both gave me presents, wined and dined me, but neither had the slightest potential as a husband.

Like my second married man, some will lie and claim they're single. If they do, how can you tell? There are lots of signals that a man is unavailable. He doesn't give you his home phone number. He doesn't see you on weekends or holidays. He breaks dates with feeble excuses at the last minute. He rarely spends the night.

The Convalescent

He might as well be married, because he's still deeply attached to his former wife or girlfriend. His heart is still broken. He's not ready to love again and won't be for some time. He's still thinking about getting her back, getting even or telling her off.

He'll date you as often as you want, but you won't have much fun with his ex along. No matter where you go or what you do or say, your every action will be colored by his ongoing involvement with his past.

If a man is still angry at his ex, still unable to spend an evening without talking about how she done him wrong, he's not ready to relate. Yet there always seems to be an "interim" woman who's willing to fill the space between his breakup and his getting well. The interim woman usually winds up as a patsy, putting up with the convalescent's condition in the hope that she will win him in the end, but she rarely does.

The convalescent usually recovers, but when he does, he moves on to a flurry of dating, and ultimately, to another woman—a new, exciting woman, one who doesn't remind him of his painful convalescence. Never play the part of the interim woman. If you decide you're interested in a convalescent, let him have his interim relationship with someone else, watch from a distance and then step in later.

The Midlife Crisis Case

Typically, this is a postconvalescent divorcé. Now that his wounds are healed, he's making up for lost time. He buys a little sports car, frets over every gray hair, shops for toupées and throws himself into a hyperactive social life. He's on every train.

The only predictable pattern followed by the midlife crisis case is that he won't date anyone less than twenty years younger than he is. If you're attracted to a middle-aged man with a younger woman on his arm, you'll know that it's a case of true midlife crisis rather than happenstance if (1) the woman is not his daughter, (2) it's a different young woman every time you see him, (3) his own friends are worried about him making a fool of himself, and (4) he's not listening to them.

If you're still attracted to him, just remember that some cases of midlife crisis last thirty years.

The Total Flake

The total flake doesn't pay his bills, can't be depended on and will always disappoint you when it comes to marriage. His life is such a disaster that there's no way he can meld it with someone else's life.

The problem with total flakes is that we sometimes think we can fix them and then they'll be perfect husbands. No way. They always regress. They can regress to drinking, taking drugs, gambling or just making endless promises they never keep, including the one to marry you.

Perpetual Bachelors

The perpetual bachelor seems supereligible at first. He comes with almost everything—dishes, silver, pictures on the wall, a house-keeper and maybe a dog. Not a thing out of place. The perfect nest, lacking only you to make it a perfect little family. You begin to imagine moving into his life.

Forget it. His house and belongings may be perfect, but he's not. He may be fun to date, but as husband material, he's a mirage. The perpetual bachelor shudders at the thought of a woman in his life on a full-time basis. He might have to share the bathroom! Or —horror of horrors—redecorate the living room!

You can tell a perpetual bachelor from an ordinary nice guy with a nice house in several ways. The perpetual bachelor protects his autonomy fiercely, hates to have his routine interrupted, barely tolerates children, never promises exclusivity and is over forty-five and has never lived with a woman. Perpetual bachelors hardly ever change. You don't have time to wait for a miracle to happen.

What to Do with/about the Time Wasters

So what do you do if you find yourself already involved with one of these proven time wasters?

1. Forget every fantasy you might have of changing him.

2. If he's a cute flake, a charming bachelor, or a gorgeous star, enjoy him as an acquaintance and, when needed, an escort to a party. Make an arrangement that leaves you free to flirt with other men.

3. Even though he's totally unsuitable, he may know someone who's just right for you. Ask him to introduce you to his friends.

CHAPTER SEVEN

Men You Don't Want to Marry

With time wasters, you're at least safe from winding up in a desperately unhappy marriage. A different group of men to stay away from are those who are marriageable but definitely unsuitable. These guys are more dangerous. Some of them will love you, love you, love you—and rush you right into a disastrous relationship. Caveat emptor.

Crazy Men

Helga, a tall, slim television anchorwoman with sharp features, intelligent green eyes and red hair, came to see me with an ugly cut on her nose. When I heard her story, I think I was more upset than she was.

"I've been telling my friends that my shower door broke and I got cut by a piece of flying glass," she said, "but the truth is Bob bit me."

"He *bit* you? On the *nose?*"

"Well, he was trying to get the ring, but I'd better start at the beginning.

"I met Bob at a car wash while I was waiting for my car to be done. He's tall, slim, really good looking and about six years younger than I am. I was flattered. We started to talk, and he asked me out to dinner.

"The first night he told me he had seen me on television and had always thought I was very attractive. As a matter of fact, he was a big fan. Usually, I'm not interested in men who want me because they've seen me on television, but Bob is different. He's deep. Committed. He served in the Peace Corps in Angola and works with underprivileged children in Watts.

"He runs and works out and has a great body.

"Anyway, he started calling me a lot, and we had these long talks on the phone. Our relationship became obsessive. I didn't think about anything but him. I bored all my friends talking about him all the time.

"We began to have dinner every night. He said he loved me. Then he gave me his grandmother's diamond ring and asked me to marry him. We moved in together.

"At first we were inseparable—always in each other's arms. He wanted to hold me and have me next to him every second. I thought this was terrific, because my ex-husband never wanted to be that affectionate. My ex was very self-centered. He spent hours and hours at his computer and never gave me the kind of time or attention Bob did.

"Bob was pushing me to marry him, but I didn't want to rush into anything.

"I was enjoying the 'being engaged' period too much. I went to lunch with my girlfriends and showed off my new diamond. Much bigger than the one my ex had given me. I felt really smug and couldn't wait to show off my new young lover to my ex and all my friends. Here I was a woman of thirty-five being adored by this handsome twenty-nine-year-old.

"Then he started to become more and more possessive, and angry and demanding. He'd expect me to take his shirts to the laundry and do all sorts of things for him.

"On New Year's Eve he'd been drinking more than usual, and

he started asking when we were going to get married. We were sitting in a booth in a hotel dining room when it happened.

"I said I didn't want to rush into marriage, and he went into a rage. He reached over and tried to pull the ring off my finger. When he couldn't get it off, he leaned across the table, grabbed me by the hair and bit my nose.

"I was so shocked I didn't know what to do. I ran out of the dining room with blood all over me. I went up to our room, put a towel and some ice on my nose and then got out of there. I found a plastic surgeon to stitch me up and give me pain pills, and he also gave me a tetanus shot.

"Anyway, Bob's been calling me. He's been all apologetic, and he says he loves me and wants me back. The reason I'm seeing you is that I want to go back.

"Everyone says I'm nuts to want to. But I saw him the other day, and the passion's still there. I've never had anyone so in love with me. I'm drawn to him. I think about making love to him all the time.

"I don't think I can stay away from him. What do you think? What should I do?"

"I think he's crazy and you should get away from him as soon as possible," I told her, "Sane men don't bite women."

"He's never bitten anyone else before. He's not a violent man. He says he's just so passionately in love with me that he can't help himself." Helga actually seemed a little pleased with the idea that a man was so driven with passion for her that he'd bite her nose off rather than lose her.

"Are you sure he hasn't left a whole slew of women behind with parts of their noses, ears, fingers missing?" I asked her. "Maybe there are women with bitten noses all through his past. Usually a man doesn't act violently just one time. It's almost always part of a learned behavior pattern he has with women.

"If you let him get away with this, you'll be doing a disservice to yourself and to every other women who comes into his life in the future. The reason he does it is because there are no repercussions. Have you thought of suing him or filing a police report?"

Helga looked stunned. How could I think of doing such a terrible thing to this man who was so sorry and who loved her so much? "Oh, I couldn't do that. I don't want to do that. I don't want to make him angrier."

Helga went back to Bob and continued coming to me for therapy. Soon I found out that Bob not only had a violent temper and was a heavy drinker to boot, but that he had borrowed quite a bit of money from Helga to finance his move into a bigger apartment so they could live together.

In spite of everything, Helga hung in. She thought she could reassure Bob enough to overcome his violence. He promised to stop drinking. He promised not to be possessive. But of course, overwhelmed by his passion for Helga, he got abusive. He called her names—"always out of jealousy," she assured me.

"He's insecure. He wants me there every day when he comes home from work. He wants to know where I am all the time. He's so different from my ex-husband, who never cared where I was or what I was doing or who I was with. We had a 'you do your thing, I do mine' relationship. I always wanted a man like Bob who really cared passionately for me."

"You *must* talk to other women in this man's life," I told her. "What about his ex-wife or his last girlfriend? Can you talk to them?" I was sure that once Helga found out Bob's passionate violence was not unique to their relationship, he'd lose a lot of his charm.

"How?"

"Easy, look in his phone book. If you're really thinking about spending the rest of your life or even another month with this man, you have a right to know if he's always been violent with women."

Needless to say, when Helga contacted Bob's soon-to-be ex-wife, she got the real story. He'd been violent many times, and that's why she was divorcing him. Bob's ex told Helga that she was lucky she didn't get more seriously injured by Bob.

Helga wanted to know if I would talk to Bob, but I told her I don't deal with nose biters or other violent people. I refused to condone her relationship in any way, not even to talk to the two of them together. I suggested that Bob get help.

Eventually, Helga talked to Bob's mother, his sister and his ex-girlfriend, and they all agreed that Bob was definitely disturbed. Although it was hard for her to accept that her passionate, adoring lover always hurt the ones he loved, she came to realize that the longer she stayed with him, the worse he got.

She moved out and gave him back the ring. Still, he followed her. He called her day and night. He cajoled and pleaded; he flattered her. They met for lunch.

"I saw him, and I want him again."

"Avoid him. Protect yourself. How much does he have to hurt you before you say goodbye for good?"

Eventually, Helga got an apartment Bob didn't know about and an unlisted phone number. Then, just three weeks after breaking off communication with him, she was tempted to hear his voice and she called his home. A woman answered.

"I'm Bob's fiancée," she told Helga. "He gave me his grandmother's ring."

Crazy men can hurt you or kill you. Crazies like Bob are not only dangerous but also seductive, because they will love you obsessively, which can be irresistible for a love-starved woman.

Some crazy men are the opposite of Bob. They can't love at all because of something in their past that makes them potentially dangerous. Does he hate his mother? Never get involved with a man who hates his mother. He's too liable to take it out on all women, you included. Does he hate his sister? Does his family hate him? Has he had lots of close friends for a long time, or is he too screwed up to be able to love someone else?

Some men are harmless-crazy, which still doesn't make them marriage material. They won't hurt you, but too much of your life is wasted dealing with their craziness.

"How on earth can a woman tell if a man is crazy before she gets involved with him? They always seem sane in the beginning," said Barbara, who had a track record of picking crazy men. Two of her husbands needed serious psychological care in institutions, and one of them still lives the life of a recluse somewhere in the canyons of L.A.

Even if a crazy man seems sane when you meet him, there are usually early warning signals.

"I guess there were some signs," Barbara finally admitted. "Harry couldn't sit anywhere but the very last row in the back of a theater, on the aisle, so that he could get out in a hurry. If we went to a movie and there were no seats in the back row on the aisle of the theater, we'd have to leave."

Women like Barbara aren't just attracted to crazy men, there's a reason those nutsy characters are attracted to them. Instead of telling Harry he was acting crazy and to cut it out, Barbara encouraged him in his craziness by actually leaving the theater with him as if it were perfectly normal to leave if you couldn't sit on the aisle in the back row. By pandering to his irrational behavior, she was unintentionally encouraging him to act even more irrationally.

Giving in to a man's every whim is a bad idea on several counts. It's bad for your self-esteem, you lose power, and you can even get a sane man to begin acting crazy if you give in to his crazy whims.

If you don't want to wind up in a relationship where a man dictates how and when you should behave in what way, then never encourage a dictator. Sane dictators become crazy dictators. Absolute power absolutely corrupts a man's mind and makes him do crazy things.

"He didn't like me to talk to him when he first came in the house," Barbara explained about her second nutcase husband. "He had to have quiet for the first hour after he came home, no television, no radio. Then he didn't want me to talk to him during dinner unless he talked to me first."

Compassionate women like Barbara are the most likely to get stuck with the nuts. A compassionate woman will always find an excuse, such as, "Lots of people don't like crowded movie theaters," or, "He hears a lot of noise at work all day, so he needs quiet at night."

Sometimes a successful older woman attracts men who need help. They are appealing in a little-boy-lost sort of way, but your chances of having a fulfilling relationship with one of these poor souls are slim. You may think you can help him, but soon you'll begin to realize that you're not making any headway and you're not getting enough back for all the giving you're doing.

There's a fine line between quirky and interesting and downright crazy. Sometimes a man who only seems quirky and interesting turns out to be mad as a loon.

The first time a guy does something bizarre, refuse to go along with it. He could be just a normal man seeing how much you'll put up with, or he could be genuinely crazy. Crazy men make unreasonable demands. Normal men also make unreasonable demands, but they're not likely to throw fits if their demands aren't granted. Never make excuses for a crazy man.

If he has fits of weirdness, meanness or tantrums, if he acts psychotic or has lots of phobias, drop him. Whatever you do, don't try to play shrink. Leave him for a professional to cure, and get on with your life.

This is not to say that crazy, irrational-acting men don't go into therapy, change and get better. Sometimes they do. But the process takes years, and you don't have years to wait. Besides, even if such a man does go into therapy and change, you may not like who he becomes, or the "new him" may not like you. Waiting for a man to get well is a losing proposition.

Men with No Integrity

If a man lies or cheats in business or in his personal life, you can bet that's exactly what he'll do as a husband.

Men who lie are often charming and persuasive. "Oh, that's just business. You're different. You know I would never lie to you, don't you honey?"

Don't buy it. Marriage is a life partnership. It's vital to be able to rely on your partner's word.

Over the course of a marriage, all men are tempted to cheat. A man of integrity will resist the temptation; a man who has no scruples will be in bed with another woman every chance he gets.

A lack of integrity can be hard to spot at first. Occasionally, a man is so amoral that he will brag about how he "put something over on so-and-so" the first time you go out with him, but more typically he won't let his guard down until after the first few dates.

Early signs of low integrity are extreme cynicism and a flip, cavalier attitude about inconveniencing other people, such as not letting someone know when he has to be late or break an appointment.

If you really fall for a man of low integrity and he promises to marry you, the best you can hope for is that he's lying about that, too.

Tall, thin, artsy-looking Michelle, a thirty-four-year-old poet and drama student from Yale, moved to California to live the Bohemian lifestyle. She went through man after man, artists and aging hippies left over from the sixties, and then she decided to change. She came to me after her attempts to find different kinds of men kept ending in disaster.

"I thought Alex was a nonartist type. A civilian. He was a doctor, and I was attracted to the fact that he was a professional, not one of my usual flakes.

"He was good-looking, dark-haired, with bright blue eyes, and he had an engaging sense of humor, but I figured out later that he was basically unstable. I noticed he drank a lot, which seemed strange for a doctor, but I didn't let it bother me at first.

"He admired me because he thought artists and writers were wonderful. I, on the other hand, was struggling to make ends meet, taking on every crazy magazine assignment I could get. Then he began to think my job as a freelance writer was so glamorous that he really wanted to be a writer, not a doctor.

"I suppose I was flattered, so I tried to help him with his writing. Soon he began working on some stupid screenplay, and he quit his job at the HMO and moved in with me. His screenplay didn't sell, and he was running out of money and using mine. I couldn't believe it. So much for doctors. I felt cheated and angry.

"I thought, what the hell, I might as well go back to artsy men. So I moved in with an actor. That was a disaster too. I discovered he liked to dress up in my clothes when I wasn't home.

"At this point, I was convinced that if a guy was attracted to me, he must be weird, perverse in some way, an ogre on the verge of a mental breakdown or something. Then I met Sam.

"We were introduced by someone, an acquaintance but no one

I knew well. Sam seemed okay, but I wasn't crazy about him. He struck me as upstanding, with traditional background and values. He owned a ranch out in the hills, miles from the insanity of Hollywood, and he raised Arabian horses for a hobby.

"When we went out or made appointments, he wasn't just punctual, he showed up early and was always impeccably dressed and well-mannered. He took me to fancy restaurants.

"I didn't think he was dangerous enough to be sexy, so I didn't go crazy for him, the way I have for men who are wilder, but I went out with him anyway because I was trying to wean myself from unstable, artistic-type guys.

"We dated for three months. We were physically affectionate but didn't make love. He thought it was because of my morals, but I wasn't that attracted to him. He was asking me to marry him.

"Here he was, a bright, good-looking millionaire who thought I was marriageable, but I thought he was boring. Then a shattering thing happened. I was reading the L.A. *Times*, and I saw it on the third page of the business section. An article that said Sam had been arrested.

"Now he calls me every day from jail. It scares me, because I find him more interesting now than before, when he wasn't a criminal. I mean he's got a big Mafia gangster for a roommate, and I want to visit him at the jail and hear all about it. I know it's sick and I need help."

Michelle had to learn to listen to her own instincts. Of course, there were signs that something was wrong with these men, but she always ignored them.

The first thing Michelle and I did was to start reconstructing her relationship with Sam. Weren't there signs that something wasn't right with him? Didn't she notice anything suspicious? Of course, but then there were the fancy restaurants, the presents, the ranch and the horses. She always ignored her suspicions, because he wiped them away with fancy footwork. Looking back, though, Michelle was able to remember that yes, there were signs.

"I guess the first thing was that I had a feeling I couldn't trust him. I thought he was lying about something, but I didn't know what. I thought it might be his age. He said he was forty-six, and I thought he was older. Something was wrong but I couldn't put my finger on it.

"He seemed to have a mysterious past. He said he had a daughter in Germany from a long time ago when he'd had an affair. He also said he was involved in espionage or something. I guess I didn't know whether to believe him, but I didn't want to find out he was lying.

"He made most of his millions in the past five or six years, awfully fast to become a millionaire. He never seemed to work when I knew him, but he was very rich. He told me he just sold his company. I didn't ask a lot of questions.

"He did tell me he divorced his wife of fifteen years after he made all his money.

"He also recently divorced a girl who was twenty-four. He married her when she was twenty-two.

"Looking back, I think I wondered why he wanted to get so close so fast and start talking about marriage when we hadn't even slept together. It was a little suspicious. But I wanted to believe him. Now I think he may have known he was going to be busted, and he picked me because he could talk to me from jail and I might visit him."

We all tend to ignore the danger signals, especially when there's something about the man that means your life problems would be over. Had Michelle married Sam, she fantasized, she would have had a life of luxury. She would have been supported, admired, everything she'd always wanted. She even would have had a non-crazy man, she wanted to think. So she overlooked the signs that something was wrong. His cloudy past. The lousy way he admitted he treated his ex. His penchant for twenty-two-year-olds. The big rush he gave Michelle. His not working.

If you've had a lot of lousy men in your life, ask yourself, why *you*? Is it because you overlook what could be wrong because you want everything to be so right?

Michelle, like many women hooked on the excitement of loving an unsuitable, romantic outlaw type, couldn't get Sam out of her mind. Despite all she already knew about him, she started to fantasize about him as being this great misunderstood business genius in jail.

"Finally, I couldn't stand it any longer. I imagined him all tan and rested from being in prison with Ivan Boesky in Lompoc, where they have the flower festival. There was my Sam, blooming with the flowers. It was all I could think about. So I decided to visit.

"But when I called, I found they had recently transferred him to Terminal Island in Long Beach, only an hour or so from where I live. I couldn't wait. I was drawn, like some scene in a science fiction movie where people are drawn to a spaceship. I couldn't sleep the whole night before, thinking about visiting him.

"I left early and got lost. Had to call the jail a whole bunch of times and try to get them to direct me, turn by turn, but they'd just reel off the directions and I'd soon be lost again. It took me three hours to find the place.

"I suppose they make it hard to find on purpose. When I got there, they made me park miles away. I hiked to the guarded entrance, and they made me fill out about umpteen forms and then told me I couldn't go in because my skirt was too short. No miniskirts.

"I reasoned. I tugged my skirt down. I begged. I explained how important it was. Finally, I demanded to see someone in charge. The guard got his boss, and I was able to talk my way in.

"It smelled terrible, of smoke and urine. It wasn't my fantasy at all. I sat in this cage with him, and he looked awful. He was pale. His hair was white where he wasn't coloring it. He didn't have a manicure. He looked depressed, and I couldn't wait to get away. I talked to him for a half-hour and all he did was tell me how he wasn't guilty, but the magic was gone. I told him I had to leave."

Sam was Michelle's last outlaw. She's now dating a landscape designer, not rich, thrilling or exciting, but also not too good to be true.

Investigating Men

You don't have to waste a year of your life dating a man before finding out that he's crazy or married or a flake or a drug addict or under indictment.

If you're getting involved with a man, if he is giving you indications that he's serious about you, you deserve to know as much about him as someone you might be hiring in a business, right? Instead, some women find themselves in a deepening relationship with a mystery man. Either he just won't tell you anything about himself and his past, or what he tells you leaves him in a vacuum —no corroborating evidence anywhere. "Oh, my folks died years ago. No, no brothers or sisters. My ex? Oh, she's crazy. I never talk to her." And so on.

If you're in such a situation (and I've had many clients who were), you are not helpless. Don't plunge ahead blindly. The first thing to do is plan a party to which you will each invite some of your oldest and closest friends. If he refuses to cooperate or claims he has no friends to invite, it's time to be suspicious.

Assuming he cooperates, make the party large enough so that it's sure to break up into several conversation groups. A barbeque, with people meandering in and out, is ideal. Make it a point to chat with a couple of his oldest friends, and ask about him. Have your closest friends do the same. Your interest in him will seem perfectly natural.

What you hear about him will either start to fill in his past or corroborate what he's already told you. If it doesn't or his friends are vague and unspecific, beware, you may have found a secret crazy.

When Jane, a thirty-eight-year-old divorcée with two children, became engaged to Dan, a doctor, he told her that he'd had some problems with his last practice, alluding to dishonesty on the part of his doctor partners. At a big engagement party, Jane and her friends found Dan's friends somewhat vague and evasive in talking about Dan. All excited about being engaged, Jane ignored this ominous red flag.

Ten months later, she came to me for counseling.

"We weren't married a month before he started screaming at me and the kids all the time," she told me. "I was terrified. I felt like I was walking on eggs and couldn't do anything right.

"He'd come home and throw a tantrum because the kitchen wasn't perfect or because the bed wasn't made the way he wanted it. Like a fool, I thought that he was so demanding because at his office he could demand anything he wanted and they'd just say 'Yes, doctor.' So I tried to create the same atmosphere at home.

" 'Yes Dan,' I'd say, and 'Yes Sir,' the kids would say, but he just got more and more hostile. I'd noticed before we got married that he always seemed to have a lot of drugs around, but I thought all doctors did. He had trouble sleeping and he'd have sweats all the time, so he took Nyquil to get to sleep at night.

"Then I caught him getting up in the middle of the night to take more Nyquil and tranquilizers. I started checking, and I found he was going through bottles and bottles of Nyquil. Plus all those tranquilizers. When I asked him if he was okay, he'd say, "I'm a physician, I know what I'm doing." But when I discovered he was using patients' names to get prescriptions from local pharmacies, I had to admit that he was a drug addict. He had bottles from all over town.

"I tried talking to one of the other doctors at his new practice, but nothing happened. I guess doctors won't do anything if one of their colleagues is on drugs unless something really horrible happens.

"I knew his mood swings were affecting his work. He was always mentioning fights with the nurses or other doctors. One day I had to take him a new shirt because he got into a coffee-throwing fight with another doctor. I was beginning to think they were all crazy and I was going crazy too.

"His partners threw him out last month, and he's trying to set up his own practice. I pleaded with him to get treatment, but he just refused and I can't take it anymore, so we're separated. My lawyer's trying to get me an annulment. I'm so upset. My life's been turned upside down and my kids have been traumatized by this madman. Now his friends tell me he's been an addict for years. Why didn't they tell me *before* we got married?"

In remembering what happened at the engagement party, Jane realized that his friends had tried to give her a clue. They knew the whole story, but what were they going to do, just blurt it out to strangers? Their vagueness signaled some sort of possible problem, Jane admitted to me, and if the same thing should ever happen in the future, she knows to go on immediate "Jerk Alert."

What's a "Jerk Alert"?

"Jerk Alert" is when you find that the man you're getting serious about is not who or what he represents himself to be or otherwise gives you reason to be suspicious. At such a point, self-preservation displaces romance. Put your plans on hold, take off your rose-colored glasses and start to check up on the guy. If he checks out okay, you'll feel good about knowing; if he doesn't, you'll save yourself endless misery and heartache.

Before you become engaged to a man, you deserve to know the following about his background and situation:

1. Full name and address
2. Social security number
3. Driver's license number
4. Birthdate
5. Place of birth
6. College
7. Military service, branch and date
8. Credit standing
9. Major debts and assets
10. Convictions (excluding minor traffic violations)
11. Major health problems (heart condition, postcombat stress syndrome, HIV positive, etc.)
12. Marital history

If a man has been forthcoming about himself and has really "invited you into his life," if he has demonstrated his honesty in little ways that you've noticed, and if his friends speak highly of his integrity, you can take his word for all the preceding with reasonably low risk. If not, especially if something has you on "Jerk Alert," you've got to protect yourself. Follow up on any information you've gotten from his friends. Let him know you're uncomfortable, that you're in love with him but that you're unwilling to commit the rest of your life to someone you know so little about. Offer to exchange information.

A man with something to hide will rarely admit it. He is more likely to blow up, accuse you of "conducting an inquisition" or some similar remark designed to make you feel guilty and then stalk off. So beware if this is the reaction you get.

Erroneous Thinking about a Man

"This time he'll be faithful." Oh sure.
"He'll treat me differently." No way.
"Most men are worse." They aren't.
"Lots of men are worse." So what?
"He'll change." He won't.
"I'll change for him." You won't.
"It's his awful childhood." Who cares?
"It's because something's wrong with me." It's not.

Older, smarter women who succeed in finding love have learned to recognize quickly when a man is impossible. They move on without blaming themselves for his shortcomings.

Don't Give Up

You've written down your criteria for a man. Add to your lists, modify them, but don't ignore them. Don't accept a terrible compromise because you're afraid you won't meet someone better. You never need to feel desperate again. Millions of nice guys are available, and they are easier to reach than you ever dreamed. In the next chapter I'll show you how.

CHAPTER EIGHT

Millions of Marriageable Men— Where They Are and How to Find Them

You're tired of singles' bars and parties. And who could blame you? Is there a line you haven't heard? Is there a stupid singles' game you haven't already played ad nauseum?

You're tired of taking pot luck among men who are "sort of" single, who only want to find a date for the evening or who really like bars and the singles' scene and want to stay just where they are. You're competing with younger, firmer women who are less demanding.

You don't have the time to stand around all evening waiting for some guy to decide you're worth talking to. You're busy. You have a life to lead, work to do, friends to see.

Ask yourself how you met the last person you dated. Was it an accident? Did you have any idea whether or not he met your criteria for a man? Or did he just happen to sit next to you in a bar somewhere?

Accidental meetings, although they can be really romantic, hardly ever come to anything for older singles. Purposeful meetings do.

If you are serious about finding a mate, skip the bars. Forget the singles' scene. And don't count on the usual advice to "pursue some activity that interests you." The problem with this advice is that you can never be sure where you'll find "Mr. Right." I never would have met my husband at a writer's group, for example; his favorite spare-time activities included dangerous sports and flying airplanes. While he still doesn't go to a lot of poetry readings and I still don't powder ski through the trees, we're very compatible in all the ways that count.

Let's face it, as you get older, a lucky accident is less likely to happen, even at a special interest group, and you have less time to wait for it. So you have to make your own luck. The way to do it is to let your maturity work for you instead of against you. Your tastes are more discriminating, your criteria are more definite and your judgment about people is better than when you were younger. So use your strengths—put yourself in the position of choosing, instead of waiting to be chosen. Within weeks, you can be choosing from literally hundreds of marriageable men.

How? By using personal ads and video dating.

I can hear your reaction. "How tacky! I couldn't do *that*! I'm not totally desperate."

I know the idea is repugnant to many of you. And I felt the same way at one time. That was before my years of research into romantic relationships, my own experience in marrying later and the experience of helping hundreds of other women do the same.

Back before videocassettes were invented, when the "personals" meant kinky sex ads in sleazy magazines, "advertising for a man" was unthinkable for most women. But times have changed, and so have the media. Today, intellectuals run personal ads in *The New York Review of Books*, and video dating is accepted by smart, upscale singles as the safest, most efficient way to meet potential marriage partners.

Stop waiting for your "prince" to come. Take action to get what you want. Use the ways that other smart women are using to find lots of men to choose from. You'll discover a time-honored, well-kept male secret: It's *fun* to do the choosing. You may feel awkward at first, but once you start, you'll feel exhilarated and empowered.

Choosing Instead of Being Chosen

Using either personal ads or video dating, you'll be amazed at the enormous pool of men you'll tap into—eligible, good-looking, nice guys who are too busy to hang out in singles' bars. You'll be in a position to filter out the kooks and the players far more easily than you can in a smoke-filled, boozy-smelling bar, and you'll never again wonder where all the marriageable men are.

Think of the process as "shopping" for a man. Like shopping for a car, a house, a new suit, except that this is the kind of shopping you do for a once-in-a-lifetime bauble, like your only fur coat ever. You'll want to be sure you get the best, but you don't want to spend the rest of your life shopping or you'll never get to wear it. Personal ads are a good way to see a lot of "possibles" fast.

Personal Ads—Busy People Use the Personals

Doctors, lawyers, accountants. Nice guys, eligible guys, sometimes shy guys advertise for love. From *New York Magazine* to *Los Angeles Magazine* and all across the country in between, respectable publications are accepting ads from men and women who want to meet.

Start by checking the personals in a local upscale publication to see how other women are describing themselves. When you do, you probably won't be able to resist browsing the men's personal ads as well. Just remember, don't believe everything you read in a man's ad and don't count on ever hearing back if you answer an ad. The odds are all in favor of those who run their own ads.

Answering an Ad

Answering a man's ad in the personals is tempting because it doesn't require the time, money and motivation that placing your own ad requires. You can dash off an answer on impulse, but the impulse rarely pays off. If you answer a man's ad, you're at his mercy, waiting to be chosen from among all the women who answer.

Men who advertise rarely answer more than one or two of the women who write. A doctor with a home in Beverly Hills said he got 450 answers to one ad in *Los Angeles Magazine*, so many that he was overwhelmed and couldn't figure out *who* to answer.

The real value in browsing through the mens' ads is to give you a sense of the kinds of men who are available and trying to reach women. Remember, what you are seeing is just the tip of the iceberg. Behind those ads are thousands and thousands of unseen readers —quality people just like you who are reading the ads but who haven't yet written one—men who are too inhibited to put their own ad in or who don't know quite what they'd write, but who know what they want when they see it. That's your target audience. Hundreds might respond to an ad from you.

After Sharon (the wedding photographer in Chapter Three) quit mooning after young Rick and got her act together, we worked on a personal ad for her to run in *Los Angeles Magazine*. She got hundreds of answers.

The ad was simple. It said, "Beautiful, sensuous, blue-eyed blonde professional photographer with dynamic personality looking for a lifetime partner, preferably Jewish, who loves to laugh. Write me and I'll tickle your funny bone."

She called me to report on her success. "I'm in heaven. It's such an ego boost! I'm getting eleven or twelve answers at a time. I just love sitting on my bed with a glass of wine and sorting my letters into piles of yes, no, and maybe. It's a good thing you had me think about my criteria for a man. I've already changed them a lot, but they've saved me hours of just comparing one guy's qualities with those of another, trying to make decisions about what I want and don't want."

Sharon sounded self-confident for the first time.

"I'm so glad I didn't have to respond to this many ads! I wouldn't have had time to run my business. Besides, just reading an ad, you don't have any real sense of who the man is. But when a guy writes, you can tell how educated he is; you can eliminate the weird ones. You can tell by his address where he lives. You can tell by his stationary how classy a guy he is. Almost all my letters came with photos, but I try not to judge by the photo alone. I don't want to be that superficial. I try to make myself read the letters first. Besides, they might not look anything like their photos.

"I try to be systematic, like when I'm going through wedding pictures at the office. I check for their age, whether they're Jewish and for key criteria of mine—like an outgoing personality and a good sense of humor. I eliminate men who refer to how much money they make or enclose a picture of themselves in front of their Rolls—all to let people know how much money they have. I eliminate men who sound too cocky, too old, too young, too serious—who only like opera or reading. I want someone to do things with, not stay home and read."

Sharon seemed to be on track. She promised to keep up her personal ad program, since it seemed to be working so well for her—and to keep me posted. Two months later, she called back.

"I ran my ad twice and it cost me about $150 each time. It's money well spent. I must have gotten four hundred letters. It was a feeling of power, just knowing all those men wanted to meet me. There were doctors, lawyers, CEOs, entrepreneurs, and CPAs all waiting for me. I got a letter from a man's cat telling about him and another letter from "Andrew's mother" telling about him. Most of the letters were thoughtful and sincere; some were like life stories, telling more than anyone would ever want to know about someone even after months of dating.

"After I sorted out the ones I wanted, I'd call and usually wind up leaving my number on their answering machine. When they'd call back, I'd say, 'Hi, you answered my ad.' Then, because they sometimes answered more than one ad, we'd go through the 'Which one are you? What did your ad say?' routine.

"If I liked the guy over the phone, I'd make a date. But phone chemistry and letter chemistry don't always translate into in-person chemistry. Some guys use pictures that are fifteen years old. Some, though, were actually cuter than their pictures. It's a real investment of time meeting all these guys, but it was fun."

"*Was* fun sounds like past tense," I interjected.

"Well, the fun isn't, but I guess meeting all those guys is. I found a guy I'm really crazy about. His name is Alan, and he's thirty-eight, a businessman. When he wrote me, he'd been answering ads in the personals for awhile but had rejected a lot of women who drank too much, were unattractive or insecure or were divorced with children. He said he was looking for someone just like me.

"Actually, Alan's letter was unimpressive, but he seemed to match my criteria. A friend took his picture in a dumb hat and sunglasses, but there was something I liked about his smile. You get very picky when you have so many to choose from, you know. There are always more than you can possibly date. That gives you a more selective feeling, knowing if you reject the guy you're out with, there are always more. So you're less likely to accept someone because you're afraid there's no other choice.

"Alan and I are together every night. He really wants to start a family. I'm sure we'll be engaged soon."

I was very happy to hear about Alan, but what Sharon said next told me she had completed the psychological transformation from loser to winner.

"And if it doesn't work out for some reason, I know there are all these other men just waiting to meet me. And meanwhile, I'm having the romance of my life."

Writing Your Own Ad

You will need three index cards. On card one, list your assets —physical, emotional, psychological, financial and social. Men want women who are affectionate and honest, so these are good qualities to start with. Men like women who look good. If you're overweight, don't say tubby, say "Rubenesque," "voluptuous," or "curvy." If you're very thin, say "slim" or "svelte," not thin.

Think about what you have to offer a man. Are you a good cook, dancer, tennis player? Advertise your best qualities. Are you loyal, loving, a lot of fun?

On card two, list the qualities you absolutely must have in a man. Leave off anything you can live without. Remember, you're trying to find all the men who might like you, so then you can choose.

On the third card, combine card one with card two, adding after what you have to offer, "looking for potential life partner who," and then adding your requirements in a man.

Be prepared to wait anywhere from three to six months for your ad to appear in a monthly magazine. Advertise in the slickest upscale magazine in your area. While you're waiting, get nice stationary and a good photo of yourself, in case you need to write back.

Video Dating—My Own Personal Story

I was thirty-nine when I began to realize I didn't want to spend the rest of my life alone and that turning forty without any prospects would be worse than not having a date for New Year's Eve. After more than ten years of writing, my work was supporting me, but even so, I was dissatisfied. Despite having dated a wonderful collection of fascinating men, I was basically going through life alone.

At about that time I had begun research on romantic relationships for my Ph.D., so I was extra busy, but still, I was lonely. I decided that a search for the most efficient ways to meet eligible men was a legitimate part of my research.

That's when I discovered something brand new—video dating —a world filled with eligible, upscale men and women committed to finding relationships and willing to pay serious money to do so. Great Expectations was, and still is, the largest video dating organization. It was too expensive for my writer's budget, but I wangled an assignment to cover it for a magazine.

Sitting in the Great Expectations office filling out a "personality profile," I felt the stigma of being unpaired in a paired society. As I checked off "over thirty-five," "never married," and "no kids," I realized I had a house, two dogs and three published books, but until then, my most committed relationship had been with Jack LaLanne's Health Spa.

Still, for some reason, I found it hard to admit that I was really there to find a relationship. I found it easier to say I was there for research or to fool around and just date.

Dating can be a good excuse for not getting close. When you're "just dating," you don't have to work things out. If a problem comes up, you just stop dating that guy and move on to the next. In fact, that's the only real problem with video dating: It makes dating almost too easy. There's always someone else if you don't like the one you're with for some reason. On the good side, you don't waste a lot of time with someone who's wrong for you just because there's nobody else available.

At first, video dating seemed a little cold, unemotional and businesslike. "Is this really what I need?" I wondered, to market myself like a product, complete with still photos, clever copy and a video-cassette interview? And, in reviewing these "prescreened, qualified and quality men" on a TV monitor, how could I get a visceral close-up, a whiff of his cologne or a look at his gait?

Even though I was outwardly disdainful of ever finding someone through video dating, I must have had hidden hopes. Carefully, I selected my best photos to go with my personality profile. Thoughtfully, I worded my essay answers. For my taping session, I wore my best color, red, and tried to be outgoing, with high energy and positive body language. Inside, I couldn't believe how nervous I was.

Once my videotape was made, the rest was fun. The dating system works well. Let's say I was stirred by Bill, code number 1534. His video presentation makes me tingle with anticipation. I tell the friendly staff, and they send Bill a notice saying he's been chosen by me, identified only as Tracy, code number 1225. Bill comes into the Great Expectations office, reads my personality profile, looks at my pictures and then watches my video in a private screening booth. If he tells the staff that he wants to meet me, we are each given the other's last name and phone number. Usually the man calls first, but there are no firm rules.

If Bill hates me at first sight, I get a little notice saying he's "not available," which could mean anything from engaged to dead to "thinks you're a dog." But no matter, I'm free to choose again and again.

At first I was like a shopaholic with an unlimited credit card in a shopping mall. I'd go in, skim the photos and personality profiles in the notebooks and pick seven or eight videos at a time to view.

Alone in my curtained booth, I played tape after tape. It was certainly exciting, having all those handsome men perform for me, vying for my attention, nervously pointing out their good features, wanting my approval. That sensation, and the opportunity to choose instead of waiting to be chosen, gave me a sense of power. I remember that feeling as though it were just yesterday, thinking, "Now, finally, I'm in control of my social life."

As the eligible men in my age group performed, I cooly critiqued each one's remarks, looking for clues about his personality. Other than Paul Newman's eyes and Robert Redford's smile, I was looking for a special tone of voice, a special chemistry.

Walter, an optometrist, says he likes the outdoors, cultural events and eating Sushi. Since he doesn't want to get involved with any of his staff or patients and he doesn't have time to go out looking, here he is. He's "into" holistic medicine, transpersonal phenomena, music and the stock market. He has sparkling eyes, a full gray-streaked beard and a nice demeanor, but I pass. He lives too far away and seems too aesthetic. I am more picky than I thought I'd be, but after all, the next one might be perfect.

I also pass on Larry and Steven. Larry, balding with a gold chain and a moustache, admits he's been hurt and, almost proudly, has "done a little hurting myself." He wants "a happy, feminine woman who is fun" (not like all those other guys who want a depressed, masculine woman who cries a lot). "A pretty, upbeat girl who makes me feel like a man," he says, adding, "Isn't that what life is all about?" I decide I hate him and hope he marries Donna Reed.

Steven is the opposite of Larry; the poor guy can hardly talk. The woman who was his wife for twenty-four years died a year ago, and he's looking for the same kind of woman. "I just want someone who'll love me as much as I loved her. But I'm not gonna run after her."

Undaunted, I spend the next two hours reading the notebooks of men from A to Z. It's hard work. Like shopping for the perfect shoes. Some of the men are obviously right for a formal occasion; others for hiking in the mountains. Some are good for looks but might be uncomfortable in the long run. Some are ugly but look warm and comfortable. Actually, a *lot* like shopping for shoes.

At first, I'm not sure what I want, so, of course, it's harder to choose. Maybe a corporate lawyer or a stockbroker? Or an artist?

Or maybe a doctor? (I found myself wishing my mother could see me now, trying to decide between dozens of real live doctors.) Yes, they have doctors, lots and lots of doctors. Doctors, it seems, haven't got time to meet women in the usual ways.

In the beginning, I choose randomly, based on looks, age, height, weight, number of kids at home and what they say on their personality profile forms and tapes. I choose a corporate attorney because he is handsome and presumably rich, and another lawyer, for the same reasons. Then I choose an expert in literary law because I think we might have something in common. I pick an orthopedic surgeon because I spotted him in the office—in the flesh—and thought he was cute.

I am filled with the spirit of the hunt. Choosing a strange man who attracts you and having him say yes is a thrill. There's the anxious waiting for him to accept. Then, talking on the phone. Finally, the meeting. The lawyers take me to the most expensive restaurants, but they are the most boring. A typical dinner conversation might begin, "Did you know I am the best corporate attorney in the country?"

The doctor is tall, four times married and has a house in exclusive Bel Air. After our first date, naturally to see the movie *Starting Over*, he says, "Why don't we move you into the guest house? You could write there." Dr. Harvey is successful and rich with a space in his life. All he needs is a resident writer to fill that one space. I could even be wife number five.

I had expected to find lots of losers who couldn't meet people in "normal" ways. Instead I found the opposite, men and women who are overqualified in the singles' market. Bright, physically attractive people who know they'll come across great on video.

A thirty-three-year-old pediatrician I met in the video dating offices said she joined because she didn't want to date men at the hospital and because the singles' scene was depressing. "I had to compete in an open meat market with beautiful nineteen-year-olds," she told me. "The most interesting people I met were other women, and we always outnumbered the men three to one. What was I supposed to do, go around shouting, 'I'm not just another pretty face! I'm a doctor!' "

A woman stockbroker told me she joined because "most of the men here are in an earning bracket comparable with mine, so I don't have to worry about fortune hunters or wasting my valuable time on unsuitable men."

It was fun sitting around the library-style tables exchanging gossip with other women about the different men we'd dated. "Oh, I went out with him," a woman next to me at the table said, pointing to a picture in the notebook I was reading. "He's a great date. We had dinner at Ma Maison (a fancy Los Angeles restaurant). He was very nice."

"Oh, don't go out with *him*," another woman volunteers, pointing to a different guy in my book. "He's really hung up on his ex-wife, and that's all he talks about all night."

Most of the men I went out with were disappointments in spite of all the prescreenings. I avoided the man who told me on the phone that his hobby was taping the spirit voices of the dead, and the one who jogged ten miles every day no matter what. But you can't find out everything ahead of time, no matter how hard you try. Sometimes it was hard to keep my face from dropping when I opened the front door. Yes, I often invited my video dates to come to my house and pick me up for the first date, even though it was not an approved procedure.

My Doberman, Poity, bit one of my video dates as soon as I opened the door; since she's usually very sweet, I didn't think I should totally disregard the dog's opinion.

Another date was a writer with whom I immediately began to argue. Too much competition perhaps. "Maybe we're just not compatible," I finally screamed at him. We laughed and agreed to call it a night. Another writer was no romantic interest either, but I did wind up editing his novel.

During my year's membership at Great Expectations, I picked more than thirty different men and was picked by almost as many. I said no to some as soon as I saw their tapes and yes to a few I later didn't like at all. I kissed a lot of frogs, but knowing that I was in the mother lode of eligible, seriously interested men, I kept trying.

Then one day I walked into the office and said, "Hi, what's new? Any cute ones?"

"Sure, this one. A real hunk." So I looked, and I picked him. And would you believe that the thirty-seventh video date I went out with turned out to be the man I'd marry?

Networking

Whether you run a personal ad or join a video dating service, you might as well "network" at the same time, since it really doesn't cost anything. "Networking" means using your friends' knowledge about you to introduce you to someone appropriate. Like "getting fixed up," but much more systematic.

Networking goes beyond the occasional phone call with a girl-friend when you say, "By the way, don't you know any nice men?" and she says, "No, if I did, I'd take them myself."

Networking to find a man means you do the same thing you would do if you were networking to find a job or to find sales leads. First, look through your personal telephone book and Christmas card list and make a separate list of every person you know who might know a man. Then make a specific, purposeful call. Be candid. Say exactly why you're calling.

Practice by looking in the mirror and saying, "I'm really ready to settle down. I'm ready to find a mate. I know you know a lot of nice people, and I'd appreciate it if you could think of someone to introduce me to."

If you've been hanging on to a bad relationship, you can use the announcement that you and whomever are no longer a couple to preface your request. If the people you call say they don't know anybody, ask them if they'd think about it and if they'd mind if you called back. You may get no responses at all on your first round of calls. You may get some later.

Single women will only give you their rejects, naturally, but that could include someone just perfect for you. You have to be careful with single men, because they like to feed women to their friends for sex and for fun, but not for marriage.

The best sources for networking are your married friends. Cultivate married couples. Get your married women friends to fix you up. They won't be saving the good ones. They'll be happy to see you married and safely mated so you're no threat. They know what makes a good husband. Your married male friends are also good to network with. They too know whether a guy is good marriage material.

Use three by five cards to keep track of any leads you get. For instance, your neighbor says she doesn't know anyone, but she'll ask her husband. He works with lots of single guys. That's a lead. Your aunt says her neighbor has a son. That's a lead. Your client says her brother's best buddy is single. That's a lead. Write down all the pertinent facts and a date to call back.

You can't expect your sources to memorize all your criteria, although some will ask you for some guidelines. When you do get "fixed up" with a man, it's up to you to qualify him as much as possible on the phone. Approach the whole thing with a sense of humor, and agree with him ahead of time to end the date fast if you don't hit it off.

Unlike running an ad or joining a video dating service, networking is a random roll of the dice. It's only advantage is that it won't cost you anything but time. And you could get lucky.

Cathy, a schoolteacher, came to one of my seminars on finding and getting a mate. She was thirty-seven, divorced, had two kids and was barely getting by. "There's no way I can join an expensive dating service," she said. "I'm on a strict budget. I can't afford to put ads in classified sections of tony magazines. I can't even join a health club."

Instead, Cathy began telephone networking, as if she were running a political campaign. She called almost everyone she knew with the same request. "I'm really serious about a relationship. Is there anyone you know that you could fix me up with?"

Everyone said no. All the men they knew were either taken or not worth having. Being prepared for this response, Cathy persisted politely. "Please just think about it, and I'll call you back in a week." In a week she called everyone back. Just one person, Agnes, a friend of her mother whom Cathy barely knew, had thought of someone.

The man was a supervisor in the office where Agnes worked. He had recently been transferred from Atlanta and had offhandedly mentioned to Agnes the problems of being single and setting up a new apartment.

Cathy called and introduced herself to Bruce, who turned out to be a never-married thirty-six-year-old bachelor. They began dating, and then living together. A year and a half after the seminar, she called me, reintroduced herself and told me she was about to get married.

Cathy got lucky, but she made her own luck. If she hadn't networked seriously, going well beyond a comfortable circle of close friends, if she had stopped just one phone call away from dialing Agnes, or if she'd gotten discouraged and given up after the first round of calls, she never would have met Bruce.

Choosing Wisely

You won't need to suffer through thirty-seven video dates, as I did, if you learn from my experience.

Become a really discriminating shopper for men. Don't waste any time at all on the losers. Use your criteria as your "shopping list." Follow your criteria, not a "come-hither" look.

Use your experience and common sense. If you've always thought of yourself as a liberal, don't get involved with an arch-conservative. My own rule of thumb is, *look for someone who is your sociological equal and your psychological opposite*. This means that if you've been to graduate school, don't try to marry someone who didn't finish high school.

This also means that if you're an introvert, don't turn your nose up at an extrovert. Two introverts are likely to live a very, very quiet life. It's important that the person you choose brings something to your life that you didn't have in it before.

A man is unsuitable for you if being with him in public is embarrassing to you. A man is a difficult match if you think he'd be at odds with your family and friends. The way to marry smarter is to look for someone who has the same values you have, and whose personality is a nice complement to yours.

First Dates

However you meet a man, here are a few rules to follow on your first date.

First of all, never go out with someone you don't like just for a fancy dinner or an expensive show. You may feel obligated, you may get involved with him and sidetracked from finding "Mr. Right." If you make a date and then realize it's a mistake, don't be afraid to cancel, as long as it's not at the last minute. Better to be honest and disappoint the guy than subject yourself to an evening you'll hate.

If you've never met the man you're going out with, meeting in a public place for "just a cup of coffee" keeps all your options open. Be "on the run" when you show up, to be pre-excused for a fast getaway if you don't like him. If you can tell in the first fifteen minutes that there's *no way* you ever want to see this person again, don't prolong the agony. Say something like, "Look, something tells me we're not a match made in heaven. It was nice of you to call me, and I'm glad we met, but let's not waste our time. I've really got to dash."

If he seems promising, tell as little as possible about yourself while getting as much information as you can from him. Don't get trapped talking about your ex'es.

If you say your ex was wonderful, he'll wonder why you're not still with him. If you say your ex was a jerk, he'll wonder if you're a jerk to have picked a jerk. Just smile and say, "When I know you better. . . ."

Talk about *him*. Flatter him with your interest in him. Concentrate on finding out if he's marriageable, if he's right for you and if you're his "type." Make sure he's marriage material. The next chapter will tell you how.

CHAPTER NINE

Inside the Minds
of Marriageable Men

A truly marriageable man is one who's ready, who believes his time has come to make a serious commitment. If you find a terrific man before he believes it's his time to make a commitment, there's almost nothing you can do to make him say yes.

When the Time Is Right, When It Isn't

Serena, an attractive thirty-six-year-old, never-married mother of an eighteen-year-old daughter, is an exotic brunette with slanty green eyes and curly hair. She exudes warmth, and people are drawn to her. Looking at her, you imagine she has all the men she wants.

"I met Max at an Innerspring growth seminar," she told me. "He was an up-and-coming Beverly Hills lawyer, and I thought he was the cutest thing I'd ever seen. He has these sparkling blue eyes and blond hair soft as a bunny's. Everyone said we were a cute couple, right from the beginning. It was easy for us to be together. We were both interested in the human potential movement, and we were kind of growing in the same direction. As we went through the stages of Innerspring training together, we started to fall in love.

"Then we started to explore other seminars and other groups. We went to trans-channelers, and took Est, and fire-walked together, getting closer and closer. I walked on fire more than fifty times, and so did Max.

"We were a part of the inner New Age circle. We were invited to parties as a couple. Everyone thought of us as a couple. Everybody could tell how good we were together. Max was able to be childlike and free, and we played together like two children."

During this time, Max began to let his law practice slide and started his own "mind power" seminars. Although he told Serena he didn't believe in marriage and commitment, he moved into Serena's house and—for a while—acted monogamous.

Together they started a radio show, and soon they were the king and queen of the Los Angeles New Age counterculture. Groups gathered every Thursday night in their living room. Guest channelers and spiritual gurus came and spoke to the gatherings, and Max and Serena became friends with people like Timothy Leary.

Then one night at a gathering, Serena began to notice other women coming on to Max, and he was acting really interested. She started to get jealous, but since they were supposed to believe in being open and loving toward all, it was very difficult for Serena to say anything to him. When she tried, she found he could talk circles around her, using lawyers' arguments to support anything he wanted to do. If he wanted to sleep with another woman, she was supposed to understand, because as he said, "I always come back to you, don't I?" And even when he stayed out all night, he would talk her into accepting it.

In the midst of these conflicts, Serena got pregnant. Max, of course, wanted her to have an abortion immediately, but she couldn't. Then, suddenly, with the worst possible timing, Max was swept away by a woman known only as the "Goddess."

"The Goddess was speaking at one of the regular Thursday night meetings through her channel," Serena told me. "We were all sitting around on the floor listening, when the Goddess announced she was going to partake of earthly desires. And she had chosen someone to be with her in this endeavor.

"She walked up to us and pointed to Max. I screamed, 'No, no.' I held on to his jacket, but he got up and walked to the front with her. I was sobbing, but all eyes were on the new couple, the Goddess and Max.

"The Goddess told Max she would give him eternal youth, make him taller, all sorts of miracles. She offered to take him on a trip to India if he would give up all his worldly possessions, including his practice and me, and just go."

Serena was devastated when Max followed the "Goddess" to India. She was pregnant, alone and overcome with jealousy. In spite of everything, she wanted him back.

"He's immature; he's an infant; I know everything that's wrong with him," she said. "But I can't imagine living without him. I'll die if he marries that woman."

I explained to Serena that she was reacting justifiably from her emotions, but that if she'd just stop to think, she'd realize that Max wasn't going to marry anyone. He had no idea what he wanted to be when he grew up, let alone who he wanted to marry. He was stuck in the Sixties, with lots of reasons why he shouldn't marry, like he "didn't want to be a part of 'The System.' " After all, no matter what Max did, Serena's life and that of her child were going to continue, and traveling around experiencing poverty in India, Max would never find the same comfort he had with Serena. I assured her he'd be back.

Just before her baby was born, Max returned, a "changed" man, he said, ready to accept the responsibility of a child—but not a wife. Serena accepted him back, had a beautiful baby boy and tried for months to convince him to get married. Now she had *two* children, an eighteen-year-old daughter and the baby, *both* born out of wedlock, and still no husband.

All their mutual friends and family put pressure on him to marry. His parents fell in love with their new grandchild, and still, Max held out.

Today, Max and Serena and the baby (now three) are still together. He adores his son and is a devoted father. But Max and
Serena are still unmarried. He still introduces Serena to people as
"my son's mother."

Why? Because Max just hasn't decided that it's his time to be
married. Perhaps he harbors some fantastical notion that one day
he'll be as famous as John Lennon, and a Yoko Ono will come into
his life.

It doesn't really matter what holds a man back. If he's not ready,
he's not ready. While Max is an extreme example, this principle
holds true for any man.

Allister, a thirty-five-year-old reporter for the features section of
a big daily newspaper and mother of two, knew she was ready for
marriage when she met Donald.

"He really came on to me," she told me. "He'd always be sitting
on my desk, flirting with me. I suppose I was flattered. After all, he's
a hotshot front page reporter on the city desk. He's tall. He's handsome. He's forty-two and has never been married.

"We went out once, and it was like we were about to start this
hot affair. I was starting to fantasize about it, and then the next
day I noticed he was acting really strange toward me at the office.
So I went right up to him and asked, 'Is something the matter?'
And he tells me he's been in therapy, working out his 'fear of
commitment problems' and can't start a relationship right now,
but will I wait six months while he finishes his therapy. What do
you think?"

Allister felt that since Donald otherwise met most of her criteria
for a man, maybe he was worth waiting for. I suggested she double-
check her judgment by listing Donald's assets and liabilities. Here's
what she found:

DONALD'S ASSETS

Likes me
Good looks
Intelligent
Hotshot reporter

DONALD'S LIABILITIES

We work together and it could be uncomfortable if it doesn't work out.

He's not ready and I am.

He probably wants kids, not an instant family.

Living with a writer who thinks he's better than I am could be hell.

He needs therapy.

His therapy might not work.

He may not want me in six months even if it does work.

He has a lot of nerve asking me to wait when I'm hardly in love with him.

It quickly became clear that Donald's assets were far outnumbered by his liabilities—the worst of which was that he simply wasn't marriageable at this time in his life. Serena told Donald she'd like to remain friends, but couldn't just wait for him. Three months later, she met Eric at a dating service and they are now happily married.

Before you get involved with a man, it's important to check him objectively against your criteria, and if you're still uncertain, make up a "balance sheet" for him. This is especially true when a man is very attractive, like Max or Donald. An arms-length, realistic assessment of a man can make the difference between being happily married like Allister or in Serena's shoes.

The Right Mindset

One of the very first things to find out about a man is whether or not he's thinking about getting married. This doesn't mean that he would "maybe like to be married some day." It means he would like to be married right now. He yearns, like you do, to be settled down, to start a family. Your best prospects are among the millions of men who have already made that decision.

How can you know? Ask. Serena could have simply asked Max, *before* she fell for him, "If the right woman came into your life, would you get married?" He would have told her all she needed to know. "Marriage? It's just a piece of paper that screws up romantic relationships." Allister, who had told Donald on her first date that she wanted to remarry, was smart enough to sense his discomfort and ask him about it.

A man's attitude about marriage is something to bring up in the very first serious conversation with him, assuming you're really attracted to him. Most women are hesitant to raise the subject, for fear of sounding too eager. They shouldn't be. Not only is it a fair subject, it's a mandatory one for anyone—male or female—who claims to be interested in a serious relationship. Besides, it's good psychology to say the "M" word and the "C" word a lot. When you do, you desensitize a man to the subjects of marriage and commitment.

The earlier in a new relationship you bring up the subject of marriage, the better. If it's one of the many "getting acquainted" questions on the first, second or third dates, a man is less likely to feel cornered, less likely to feel you're hinting, really asking him about *now*, and *you*. Whenever you bring it up, don't make it sound like you're proposing to him. Don't ask, "Do you want to get married?"

Instead, keep it light and conversational. Tease him a bit, even. "You've said you'd like to have kids. I don't know. Even if you met the right woman, I bet you wouldn't want to get married and settle down. You seem like you still have a lot of playing around to do." Make it easy for him to respond either way. If he's reached "his time" to get married, he'll tell you. "Oh, no! I've run around all I want. I'm really ready to settle down."

If he says, "Well, I am enjoying being single" or anything that indicates he's not really ready, *believe him*. Whatever you do, don't waste time waiting for an antimarriage man to change into a promarriage man. It's like expecting a prolifer to become prochoice or a Republican to become a Democrat. Sure, it happens, but the odds in your favor are pitiful.

Stay focused on your objective. Find out right away if a man believes in marriage and wants to be married. When you start choosing only from among men who are ready to be married, your

chances of getting married will leap past those of other women—
no matter how attractive—who are nonselectively dating.

The Right Fantasy

Inside the mind of a truly marriageable man is a fantasy image
of his future wife. Sometimes the image is hazy, sometimes it's
crystal clear—but it's there.

If you're short, dark and intellectual and his fantasy is a tall
blonde who plays tennis and never argues, he may date you, even
romance you (just to try "something different"), but you're wasting
your time if you think he's going to marry you. You're never going
to be his tall blonde fantasy, no matter what you do.

For instance, let's say you're the wild, outgoing type and you
meet a guy who makes it clear he prefers the quiet, demure,
"feminine" type. So you try to act sweet and passive and quiet,
and what happens? If he falls for it, you won't be able to keep
up the act, and eventually he'll become disillusioned. If he doesn't
fall for it, you're going to feel especially stupid for trying so hard
to be what you're not.

So the real trick is to *find a man whose fantasy you fill*, instead
of trying to fill the fantasy of the man you've found.

If you're dark and sultry, don't bleach your hair and break a leg
learning to ski just to live up to someone's Nordic skier fantasy;
stick with men who go crazy for sultry Mediterranean types. If you're
tiny, don't try to make a man happy who's always wanted long legs.
Date guys who love their women petite.

To a large degree, fitting a man's "type" will happen automatically if you only choose among men who want you. Still, guys will
go "out of type" just to experiment. Even if a serious relationship
develops with an experimenter, he will always wonder what he's
doing with someone so different from what he always wanted. He'll
never give up wanting his real fantasy. So a "fantasy check" is always
worthwhile, even if a man seems enamored of you.

How do you find out what a man's secret fantasy woman is?
Here's how to get it out of him on the first date. You say, "You

know, I'm surprised you asked me out. I would have thought your type was a . . . [describe someone very different]." He may agree, saying, "Well, actually, I'm usually attracted to . . . [someone different from you], but you just seemed so interesting." If so, ask him, "Tell me about your last few girlfriends. What were they like?" If they're all totally different from you, this guy's a longshot unless he's determined to change his luck.

He may say, "Nah, I don't have a type. I play the field." If so, tease him some more. "Come on, all guys have a type. I bet your last three girlfriends were brunettes [or whatever's different from you]."

The ideal response (if, say, you're a bit overweight) is, "But you *are* my type! I've always been wild for huggable women. I can't stand skinny chicks, with bones sticking out!" If his response is instantaneous and congruent, you can probably believe him.

If you discover that you are indeed close to a man's fantasy woman, then you can be sure that your odds of marrying him are much greater than your odds of marrying someone whose fantasy you don't fit.

The Right Woman for Children

A man who marries and wants to have children will look for different qualities in a woman than a man who has had six kids and now wants a wife to help him with his political career.

When an older man becomes ready to marry and wants children, he usually gives up airheads and starts to pay attention to brains and other qualities he's hoping for in his offspring. "After all, I don't want to have dumb kids," one man told me bluntly. Other men said the same thing in different ways. "I want a woman I can depend on to take care of my kids." Often a man has a definite idea of what he wants his kids to look like. "I picture myself with lots of blond surfer-type kids, just like I was as a kid," a California investment banker told me.

It's important to find out a man's fantasies about children as soon as possible. Here again, the best way is simply to ask him— as early in the dating process as possible. If you don't fit the picture he has for the mother of his future children, chances are he won't marry you.

If he doesn't want children at all, that presents a whole different problem. When a marriageable man doesn't want children, he's going to be rightfully wary of any woman who hasn't already had children, since he knows she's bound to feel the mothering urge sooner or later.

Jennifer and Ken were introduced by good friends. Jennifer, age forty, owns her own public relations company, is a high-energy, high-fashion woman with lots of pizzazz. Ken, a high-powered business consultant, had many of the same interests. "I couldn't be happier," she cooed when she first told me about Ken. "I think this one is a real possible."

Jennifer hadn't had a "real possible" since her ten-year marriage ended when she was thirty. The marriage was so bad that she thought she'd never marry again. "I was unhappy for the whole ten years. We didn't communicate at all. All he did was complain about me, and we hardly ever had sex. With Ken everything is different. He makes me his princess.

"Over Thanksgiving we went to Napa to the wine country, and afterwards he sent me roses just as a 'thank you' for going with him. He really swept me off my feet."

Jennifer, who always said she wanted to have two kids of her own, was especially happy about Ken's four young children from his previous marriage. "Even if I don't have kids of my own, I'll be able to mother his," she told me. "It's perfect."

For more than a month, Jennifer and Ken were together. They played tennis; they skied; they jogged. Their high-energy lifestyles seemed to mesh like two sides of a zipper. Then suddenly it was over. Jennifer was stunned when she called me.

"Ken just told me that he couldn't handle the guilt he would have for not giving me children of my own, and with four young children already, he didn't want any more. He said it was too big an issue to sweep under the carpet. We could just be friends.

"We were so good together. It makes me angry that he made that decision all by himself and then announced it to me!"

Later, Jennifer admitted that maybe Ken was right, that having kids of her own *is* important to her, that maybe she was wrong in avoiding the issue at the beginning of a relationship.

"I guess I swept it under the carpet before. But no more. My experience with Ken was too painful. I've changed my criteria—a man's willingness to have kids is right up there at the top of the list. And I'm not bashful about asking a man, especially if he says he's 'already had a family.' I just come right out and and say, 'Well, would you ever have more? What about adopting?' I don't care if that's off-putting. Better to scare a guy off on the first date than to get your heart broken later."

The Right Woman to Take Home

When a man gets serious about a woman, one of the first things he worries about is introducing her to his family. If he feels that he wouldn't be able to take a particular woman "home to mother," he's probably going to rule her out as wife material.

In any group of women, Amy stood out. She was thirty-five, with a great figure and long, straight blonde hair that hung halfway down her back. She always wore sandals and peasant skirts, and she didn't own a bra. She especially loved to show off a tiny spider tattoo between her breasts, and she wore some decolleté outfits to emphasize her free spirit.

Bill, an engineer, looked like a computer nerd. Short hair. Polyester suits. He was fascinated by Amy's spontaneity and lack of inhibitions. She taught him sex acts he had never dreamed of, and he found her irresistible, for awhile.

Amy and Bill lived together for eight months, but the relationship was doomed. While they were together, Bill made several trips home to Vermont to visit his family. He always left Amy behind in L.A.

Each time, Amy would make an excuse for him. "Oh, Bill didn't think they were quite ready for me," she joked. Inwardly, though, she was hurt. The truth was that Bill could never take Amy home to his conservative New England parents.

When the relationship came to an end, Amy was doubly upset. "I was really in love with him. I could have been a wonderful wife for him, too," she told me, "but he just wouldn't give me a chance. And what's worse, I saw the handwriting on the wall months ago. I just refused to believe it."

If you are interested in a man who can't take you home or finds your appearance embarrassing in front of his friends or family, drop him. He'll never marry you. Marriageable men want to be proud of the women they choose. They want to show them off to their family and friends.

After wasting nearly a year in a hopeless relationship with Bill, Amy had learned her lesson. Her next man was an artist, with kooky friends and an accepting, supportive family. His parents were already used to his eccentric friends, and taking Amy home to mother was no problem for him.

The Right Way to Protect His Assets

Often, the man you find has already got a house, investments and other property. Whether he's worked hard to amass his assets or whether he's inherited them doesn't matter. His first concern may be whether you're a fortune hunter and whether you'll take everything from him if the relationship doesn't work out.

A man who has already suffered losses from a divorce is especially cautious. If his ex-wife is living in the house he once owned, he'll be doubly concerned. Even if he doesn't say anything, you can be sure he's thinking about it. For a lot of men, fear of commitment is really fear of losing their assets.

Henry, the never-married, thirty-five-year-old heir to a substantial family fortune, told me, "I'm willing to support a woman in a luxurious way, but I'm not willing to share all my property with her. You know that part about 'with my worldly goods I thee endow. . . .' Well, that's a bunch of bullshit as far as I'm concerned."

So if you meet a man with a lot of property, you should always show him in subtle ways that you're not greedy, that you don't need him for his money because you're making money on your own and that you love him for himself, not his money.

We'll come to the subject of handling financial concerns with premarital agreements in Chapter Twenty, but the point here is that a man with lots to lose is more likely to want a long engagement than a man with no assets.

The Right Mating Ritual

A man who's ready to marry will often have preconceived ideas about how quickly he will marry after he meets a woman. If he's been through a disastrous divorce and he attributes his misfortune to rushing into his last marriage, he'll be slow to commit and very set on a long engagement.

Or he may be a real romantic, with a fantasy elopement all worked out in his mind: a first-class flight to Hawaii, arriving just in time to get married at sunset on the beach at Mauna Kea. If he decides you're "Ms. Right," off you go.

How a man feels about the "mating ritual" is actually one of the easiest things to find out from him. Almost everyone has an opinion on elopement versus conventional marriage ceremonies, long versus short engagements. If you let the subject come up naturally, for example, in connection with friends who are getting married, you can discuss it without him feeling cornered.

You: "Isn't it romantic? They surprised everyone by sneaking off to Mexico. A Mexican marriage *is* legal, isn't it?"

Him: "Sure it is. They're not only romantic, but smart, spending their money on a great trip instead of blowing it all on a fancy reception."

His comments about your friends are a good indication of how he would like to handle the same subject.

CHAPTER TEN

Attracting a Man—What Works, What Doesn't

Most old, overused, easy-to-see-through attempts to trap a man don't work. They backfire, making you seem desperate, needy and inappropriately giving or anxious. Part of being successful in finding a mate when you're older is being smart enough to give up these tactics, and realizing that the man you want has seen these pathetic ploys over and over again. Trying one just puts you in the "Ho hum, another woman trying to catch wonderful me" category.

Leaving Your Stuff

Leaving things at his house "accidentally on purpose" doesn't work. Nor does it work to leave things in his car, office or pocket. He just figures you're trying to trap him into seeing you again to get your property back. All women try this, and all men know exactly what it means. Leaving something at a man's place, unfortunately, is such an overused trick that even if you leave something by accident, he'll think you did it on purpose.

Acting Wild

You've probably envied those women who look and act wild and attract men like bees to honey. If you're thinking of trying the same, just remember that the guys you'll attract may not be the ones you want. Most grownup men have learned to be afraid of certain things in a woman. Even a man who isn't intimidated by wildness in a woman worries:

Will she get me into a fight in a bar?

Will she do something so embarrassing that she'll get me thrown out of my law partnership?

Will she insult my buddies, my boss, my mother?

Will she get me arrested or in other trouble?

Will she spend all my money?

Will she chase away all my friends?

Obvious Game Playing

Men expect to be flirted with, but not lied to. You should know that the "number one turnoff" reported in a recent, large-scale survey of marriageable men was "a woman who can't be trusted." So if you lie to a man and he catches you, it's all over.

Rather than lie about something, don't say anything at all. You don't have to tell him everything. It's better to tell a new man as little as possible. Be mysterious; don't be a liar or a game player.

Cutesy Cards

Sending him cutesy cards before he tells you he loves you is a definite no-no. The cards remain behind as hard evidence of you flinging yourself at him, potential embarrassment for years to come. If you just can't resist, hold yourself to a standard Christmas card, with *no notes*, just your name. Valentine's Day and birthday cards are out unless you're in a relationship with him.

Expensive Gifts

Why do women do this? One-way gift giving, especially with expensive gifts, just tells a man that you're a masochist, open for unrequited love. It also puts a monetary value on the relationship, and love is supposed to be priceless.

Joan Collins learned this the hard way when she went through the ugly divorce from Peter Holmes. Even when she gave him everything, he couldn't resist "Passion Flower." Who wants a man who can be bought, anyway?

Needing a Rescue

Any ploy that makes you seem helpless won't work. A man who is looking for a life partner doesn't want a basket case—that is, unless you've run into the particular kind of man who has a need to rescue women. The trouble with this kind of man is that he has to keep rescuing, so if he rescues you and then you're okay, he loses interest. To keep his interest, you will have to stay on the brink of some kind of disaster, always needing help from him.

If this sounds somewhat appealing, in an *Indiana Jones* meets *Perils of Pauline* kind of way, just think about what happens if you get used to living your life like this and then he finds a damsel in deeper distress.

I counsel a woman who's the mistress of a very wealthy man. For her own sanity and self-respect, she'd really like to become self-sufficient and emotionally stable, and she's capable of it, but she can't because her "mentor" would then lose interest.

Clutching at Him

We women clutch at men in different ways. We can't seem to help ourselves. We all want to control the source of our pleasure. Maybe it's instinctive. Try to curb this instinct.

Try not to clutch physically. It's all right to show affection in public once in a while, but don't be a constant *clinger*. Let go of his arm occasionally.

Likewise, try not to clutch socially. A woman is clutching when she says, "When am I going to see you again?" *Never, ever* say, "When am I going to see you again?" Don't sound like an empty life. Be unavailable now and then. People who aren't desperate are un-available *sometimes*.

Try not to clutch emotionally. Don't whine about what's wrong with your life or what you need or what would make you happy. Don't say "I love you" first, trying to obligate him into saying the same. Don't talk about getting married before and after sex.

Calling Him

You've seen someone you think you'd like. Or, you've been out with him a few times. You may have even been to bed together. You're *dying* to call him, to find out if he's still interested, or if he ever will be, and you're groping feverishly for some excuse. Maybe, you rationalize, he's just forgotten about you and your call will jog his memory. *Stop*. You're about to make a major error.

The minute you call a man, you give him the upper hand in the relationship. You lose power. He thinks, "Aha, she's after me!" For best results, follow these rules:

Rules for Calling and Asking Men Out

1. Postpone calling as long as you possibly can. Think about something else. Get away from the phone. Call a girlfriend for support. Most of the time, you're better off *not* calling a man. No matter what you say, he's going to think you're chasing him.

2. If you *must* call, be prepared. Rehearse ahead of time what you're going to say. Be peppy and sound happy, like you're having the time of your life or are about to—that way he'll think he's missing something. *Never* call a man when you're down.

3. Always have a purpose, a reason for calling. Be prepared to get off the line gracefully and quickly if you don't get a warm

reception. "I'm on my way out, just wanted to catch up with you. Let's talk sometime soon."

4. If you call once, that's *it* until he calls you. If you call a man more than once without him returning your call or asking you out, you look too eager, too needy and too desperate.

5. If you want to ask a man out, be specific. Not, "Uh, hi, there's this movie I'd, ah, like to see sometime," but rather, "My boss gave me two tickets for the Lakers game Thursday night. Would you like to go?" Or, "I just closed a big deal and the client gave me a bottle of Dom Perignon. I hate to drink alone. Would you like to come over and share it?" Or, "I'm having some friends over next Saturday, would you like to join us?"

6. Most men are flattered when a woman asks them out. Others are a little flustered. So be prepared to tell him the details. Tell him the time, the dress, the arrangements. "I'll pick you up at eight. Dress is casual. Don't worry about a thing. I'll take care of everything." Or, "Just show up. Dress is casual. The party starts at eight. They're only serving light hors d'heurves, so you might want to eat something first." Men worry a lot about whether they're going to be fed and how much.

7. Be prepared for rejection. If he says no, get off the phone cheerfully and quickly, as if you were going to go to the next name on the list. Don't whine. Never beg. Don't sound depressed.

8. If he says yes to the date invitation, don't expect him to pay. In the world of grownups, if you invite someone out, they expect you to pay. If you invite a man to your house, he expects sex. If you don't want to have sex, then don't invite a man to your house alone.

9. Never ask a man out twice in a row. If he rejects your invitation, don't ask again. It's his turn to ask next if he's interested.

10. Don't think that you can obligate a man to take you out because you take him out. That's not the way it works. So just enjoy the evening. It's a gamble, the way a man gambles when he takes a woman out. He may or may not want to see you again. Asking him out just gives you a chance to show him what he could have should he so desire, so don't ask him unless you're prepared to show him your best; you may only get one shot.

Tactics That Work

All the tactics that really work share a common characteristic: They make the man look up to you in some way. He is enticed instead of pestered, charmed instead of bored, and he sees how wonderful you are instead of how pathetic you are.

Happiness

One of the surest ways to attract a man is to be happy. Even if you're miserable, act happy. Nobody wants an unhappy woman. But if you're happy, men are irresistibly drawn to you, wanting to share your happiness. Only sickies want to get close to unhappy people.

Admiration

Let him meet other people who admire you. His interest in you will be validated, and he'll want you because you'll seem more valuable. He'll find it flattering for you, the one who is admired, to admire him—and he'll find it very seductive.

Indifference

When all else fails, indifference works. Have you ever noticed how the men you care least for try the hardest? They call. They send cards. They wine and dine you, shower you with attention and gifts. They want to make dates way into the future. So one technique that always gets a man's interest is to act slightly indifferent.

Indifference works best if you first act interested and then act indifferent. Indifference also works if he's interested and drifting away. Forget about "try a little tenderness." Instead, try a little indifference.

Getting In Tune with Him

Liking what he likes and emphasizing the similarities between you will always get you further than emphasizing your differences. If he likes himself and has a healthy sense of self-esteem, he will like you if you're on the same wavelength he is. We all tend to trust others who are like us. He will trust you more if you seem like "his kind of people."

If he talks fast, for example, step up your own rhythm to get "in sync" with him. Doing this sends subtle but powerful signals that you agree with him and approve of him. He'll be instantly comfortable with you and will probably not even know why.

This doesn't mean that you have to agree with him on everything. To the contrary, once you've established this degree of rapport, you can disagree on issues that are important to you without endangering the whole relationship.

Providing Romance

Men are suckers for romance, even more than we women. The trouble is that men don't understand exactly what romance is. To a man, romance is a magic occurrence—uncontrolled, unpredictable and unexpected. Like in the movies. Men find it hard to think in terms of *planning* romance, but if a woman plans a romantic encounter, they react enthusiastically.

Romance the way women like it—soft, slow, sensual—works with a man, too. We sometimes get in trouble with men when we approach them as buddies because they start to see us as one of the boys instead of as a woman. So if there's a man you want to be romantic with, don't slap him on the back. Instead, touch him gently. Stroke him. Go sailing under the stars or walking on the beach in the moonlight.

Being Unpredictable

One way to keep a man's attention is to do the unexpected. Show him new things to learn about you, new revelations of how wonderful you are. Do something different, if for no other reason than to be unpredictable. Remember to be unavailable occasionally. Take a little time away just when your relationship is at its peak of passion, so he'll be sure to miss you.

Finding Something Special about Him

Find a special quality about him that isn't obvious, one that others have failed to appreciate. Then let him know that you appreciate that special quality. If you really care for him, you must have noticed something.

Maybe only you appreciate that he has the handsomest legs you've ever seen. Or the sexiest shoulders, or the most adorable little toes. Or maybe only you appreciate that inside your mild-mannered accountant beats the heart of a romantic adventurer. Or only you see the inner strength in your soft-spoken engineer. Find that one special quality, and he'll have to keep coming back to you to have it appreciated.

Sex: How Soon, How Often, How Kinky?

How Soon

Of course you know not to have sex on a first date. You don't want him to think that you have sex with everyone on the first date, and you'll want to be sure he's the kind of man you should be having sex with.

Some women have been told that they shouldn't have sex with a man until they have a commitment or a ring on their finger. So these women lead a man on until he's panting, and then they say they won't sleep with him without a commitment. The guy feels like he's being manipulated, and he is. Men aren't stupid just because they're horny. Don't ever tell a man commitment first, then sex. When sex gets that transactional, the relationship is in trouble.

On the other hand, don't be easy. There's nothing wrong with letting a man know that he turns you on and you might enjoy going to bed with him after you know him better, but not tonight.

Nevertheless, things happen. If you're gotten yourself in a situation with a man where both your juices are flowing and your hormones are careening through your body and he touches you and you feel waves of heat and electricity, how can you stop? Not very easily. And if he knows the feeling's mutual, he'll think you're some kind of game player or a terrible prude if you stop.

So what do you do if you can't stop? You say, "I don't know what's happening to me. I can't stop myself with you." He wants to feel special. He *wants* to believe you when you say, "I've never gone to bed with anybody this fast in my life."

Afterwards you might say, "I don't know what you did to me, you just swept me away. I never do this sort of thing." Keep a straight face.

How Often

Don't worry if he seems to want sex day and night. During the courting stage, that's normal. What else does being swept away with passion mean? Don't worry that you'll have to have sex with him every hour for the rest of your life. You won't. It'll wear off after you've been married a while.

How Kinky

Don't do anything you feel uncomfortable with. Do try to develop some special technique or unusual sex act that just the two of you do together. The more unusual, the better. That way he'll be more bonded to you, more likely to stay, knowing how awkward it would be to ask a strange woman to do whatever it is you do. An unusual sex act can be a delicious secret, shared only by the two of you.

Staying Sexy

Act "as if." Sure, you know you're not the same as you were when you were twenty-two. Your body may not be as good, but your mind is better. So use your mind to act "as if." Tell yourself, "I'm gorgeous. I'm sensual. I'm a lusty, sexy woman."

Recently, I counseled June, who came in from out of town to see me. She didn't want her husband to know about it. She was thirty-seven, quite a bit overweight, built like an upside down pear with giant breasts and tiny hips. She had the kind of figure us right-side-up pears always admire.

Actually, her face, with large brown eyes and framed with soft blonde hair, was quite lovely, but her body posture said it all. She sat with her shoulders hunched like she had the weight of the universe on them. She looked down. Her feelings showed.

"I've gained a lot of weight since the last baby came, and I don't feel very attractive anymore. My husband stays out all the time, and he doesn't look at me the way he used to."

We worked together on a plan for her. It had a lot to do with acting "as if."

"How would you feel if you were forty pounds lighter?" I asked June. "Oh, I'd feel better," she looked up.

So I asked her to close her eyes, and we would imagine how she would be if she were thin. We took imaginary pounds off her, five pounds at a time. With every five pounds of imaginary weight, June sat up straighter. Before my eyes she changed. Her shoulders went back, her breasts stood out, she arched her back and tossed her hair.

As I took June on this imaginary trip back to the time when she felt good about herself, she began to feel good about herself again in the present. She started to feel the same feelings she'd felt before she'd gained the weight.

Using her mind alone, June transformed herself from a discouraged blob into a sensual, sexy woman right before my eyes. Then, to seal the deal, we anchored her good feelings.

"Now make a fist," I told her. "Feel how powerful you are now. Feel the sexy new you.

"Whenever you begin to feel the old bad feelings again, you'll be able to make a fist, shut your eyes and become the June we both know is in there. You're still the same person no matter what you weigh. That person is inside you, not gone. You can reach in now and have the power to act as if you were thin, no matter what."

June still had problems at home, but she began to focus on them more clearly. She felt good about herself.

If you've gained weight or if something is less than perfect in your life and you're not allowing yourself to feel as attractive or as sexy as you used to, you can use the same technique I taught June. Just talk yourself through it, and act "as if" your problems were gone. You can do it, because the truth is, you have the potential to be sexier than ever.

One of my personal friends, Sally, is a zoftig yet very sensual woman of fifty who's always had a man in love with her. Her secret is simple: "I don't feel fat," she says. "I think of myself as voluptuous, and I sure know how to turn a man on."

As a mature woman, you have the advantage of experience—with life, with men, with sex. You have an advantage over those young cute things just coming of age who are insecure about their sexual ability. You, on the other hand, have had time to learn how to enjoy sex. You know how to appreciate and contribute to the sexual happiness of your man. You may even be able to teach him a thing or two.

Dating Rules

Always act happy and busy, like there are lots of men who want you.

Always give a little less than he does, so you don't give too much and seem needy.

Never call him without a good reason, and only leave one message, never two.

Only say "I love you" if he does.

Show your willingness to pay your share.

Be unavailable once in a while.

Respect him and his belongings. Don't try to control him.

Act healthy, not whiny or sickly.

Let go of his arm in public now and then to show your self-assurance.

CHAPTER ELEVEN

Managing the Relationship

Starting Right

One way women can apply the experience they've gained in other parts of life to their love lives is to recognize that the beginning of a love relationship is much like the beginning of a business partnership. Both parties are skeptical at first, especially if you've been wounded at love before. If you're determined to be smarter at love this time, neither of you is anxious to jump into a relationship until you're sure you know who you're "getting in bed with." Both of you will want to negotiate carefully before you make long-term commitments.

As in any negotiation, the person who needs the deal the most is always at a disadvantage. So even if you feel you're the one who needs the romantic deal the most, don't show it by letting impatient actions make you seem too eager.

Susan, a thirty-two-year-old artist, met Allen, a real estate agent, when she was looking for a house to rent. They'd only had one date when she came to see me.

"Allen is exactly the man I've been looking for," she told me.

"He's everything I want, we had a great time together, and I felt that he liked me a lot, except he's never called back. It's been over a week now. I'm beginning to wonder if I'm not his type. Maybe I should call and tell him I really like him, and ask him if he's got any real interest in me. I can't stand not knowing."

If Susan had been aware of the principles in this book, she wouldn't have had to come to me. I explained that calling Allen would be foolish. Instead, Susan employed the tactic of indifference, and let time be her ally. She was glad she did. Five weeks later, Allen called her, anxious about whether or not she was still open to seeing him.

"I've been dating a lot of women," he told her, "but I just couldn't get you off my mind."

Never blurt out to a man that you're serious about him until he shows interest in you. There's nothing more deadly than pushing at this delicate stage in a relationship.

If you can wait, just a little, you can save yourself embarrassment and allow a man's feelings about you to develop naturally. Give yourself time to find out about a man before you decide you want him. Don't start fantasizing about marrying someone you just met. Acting impatiently can chase away a good one or throw you into the arms of someone who turns out to be an undeserving lout.

Another negotiation mistake women make in relationships is to cut off all other men the minute they meet one they really like. Even worse, they then tell the man what they've done. I can't tell you how many women have come to me about a man not being attentive enough or even walking all over them and have said, "Oh, he knows I'm not seeing anyone else"—as though there were no connection.

Voluntary monogamy is a sure sign of someone who has lost power in a relationship. A woman will take this step out of some mixed-up fear of losing the man if she doesn't, even though *he's* made no commitment whatsoever. She's ready to forsake all others without even being asked, just to prove her love, hoping this gesture will somehow bond him to her. All it does is make him feel in total control of the relationship.

I always tell these women, "If you were starting a new business and you had only one client, would you let that client know he was the only one?" The answer is obvious. Of course not. You'd want to seem busy, in demand, wanted.

If he asks, "Are you seeing anyone else?" Just say sweetly, "Oh, I have a lot of friends I do things with. I'm sure you do, too."

The minute you let a man know he's the only one, you ask for trouble, unless you have discussed your relationship seriously with him and have arrived at a mutual agreement to be monogamous. Never, ever tell a man he's the only man in your life unless he's told you you're the only woman first. He may not even be available for that honor.

The "Key Times" Availability Test

How can you tell if a man is really available? Being "available" doesn't mean he's not dating. Don't be discouraged if you find a man you absolutely adore and he's already dating one or more other women. Of course he is. If you find a good one, other women have too. The real question is whether he's so involved with, or committed to, another woman that he's ineligible for you.

The way you find out is by his availability during the "key times" that are critical to a relationship. Don't worry if he can't see you every night at first. But a man who won't see you on weekends and holidays and won't stay all night with you is not available, no matter what he says or what you'd like to believe.

This test, of course, immediately flushes out married men, who can often arrange to stay overnight but always disappear on week-ends and holidays. It also flags men with so many women on their string that the only position open is pinch hitter—you get every fifth weekend, and you won't know until the last minute. "Key times" availability is an especially important test for men with "roommates"—as in, "Oh, she doesn't mean anything to me, we're just roommates."

If a man is flunking the availability test, keep your suspicions to yourself until you find out exactly what's going on. If you tell him you suspect he's not telling you the truth and he's lying, he'll just be more careful with his cover-ups. Or if he's not lying, your accusations could ruin the relationship.

When I first started dating my husband, he told me his nineteen-year-old daughter was going to be moving in with him for a while. "Oh sure," I thought. "I've heard that before." When I saw her the first time, blonde, beautiful and built, I was even more suspicious. But luckily, I didn't say anything, because it turned out that he was telling the truth.

The "key times" availability test also will expose men who are ineligible for other reasons you might not even be thinking of. Like a man who's trying to start a new business. Entrepreneurs can rarely make plans for weekends and often can't keep dates reliably during the week. They don't have time for a satisfactory relationship with you, because they already have a love they're totally devoted to.

Men who are caring for an aged mother, sister or other relative are commendable, but if this other commitment in their lives makes them flunk the "key times" availability test, they're just not good marriage material.

Sometimes, the best marriage material is right under your nose.

Changing Friendship to Love

Your best marriage prospect could be a man you already know. Someone you work with. Maybe even a good buddy, someone whom you've always liked and admired as a friend but never considered seriously as a romantic interest. For him to see you as a possible love interest and start changing friendship to love, you have to let him see you in a new light.

Liz, an executive at a theatrical agency, was more than ready to marry and had access to lots of attractive men, but her contacts with them were all business-related. The men were always complimenting her on her sharp mind, keen judgment and always-together look, but none ever approached her on a personal basis.

"I was thirty, just ending a long relationship that didn't work out, when I was offered my job in L.A. At first, I dated lots of

Hollywood types. Since I worked for a powerful agency, I was in demand, but I never knew whether a guy was interested in me or was hustling me for business purposes. Usually, it turned out to be a business hustle.

"By the time I was thirty-two, I was really getting worried. I was starting to tell myself. 'Well, maybe I'll never get married.' I was trying to resign myself to it. I'd lie in bed at night and worry that I wouldn't have children and that my biological clock was running out. 'I'll be a career woman,' I told myself. 'I'll have important jobs, do great things.' I wasn't very convincing."

I told her, "You have access to the most eligible guys in the city. You have lunch with them, meetings, conversations. Why not one of them? Maybe only the hustlers are asking you out, and the nice guys aren't because they respect your business relationship. What you need is for the good guys to see you in a different setting, outside business, without having to ask you out."

I suggested that she have a couple of semibusiness Sunday brunches at her house, inviting the men she knew who liked her, and other women too, but the men would basically be there for her. On her home territory, I figured, they'd be sure to see her as a person. And it worked, because one of them was Michael.

"I remember the day he came to my brunch, and when he left with everybody instead of staying afterwards, I felt sad," she told me later. "I figured he didn't like me after all. Then, a few days later he called me to go out to the Malibu Grand Prix, where you race little cars around a track.

" 'My sister's in town,' I told him, and he said, 'Bring her along.' He was great about my kid sister, and we got a lot closer that night. Then he invited me to a cookout at the beach, only we went by his place so he could change and we never left.

"We had actually known each other for months. The first time we met was when I was asked to meet with him and a director about a book. The director was late, and Michael was entertaining me while we waited. We talked about books, and I was surprised to see how much he read."

That was in August. Liz had the brunch in February. She and

Michael were dating seriously in March and living together six months after that. They got engaged in December and married the following June. Liz was pregnant a year later. She married one month before her thirty-fifth birthday and will have had her second child one month before her forty-first.

Like Liz, you may work with some interesting men but not be able to make contact on a more intimate level. Perhaps you could have brunches, or barbeques, or cocktail parties. Invite men you think like you in business, and who match your criteria. You'll cement business relationships and have a good chance at meeting the man you'll marry.

Drawing from a pool of men you already know in business helps ensure that you're not wasting your time with someone who doesn't match your criteria. You can prequalify each man as to availability and what he's like, at least in business. You can invite other women who are nice, but who won't outshine you. You can stack the deck and play on your home court. Once you find your man, then your next step is to make sure he feels loved.

What Makes Him Feel Loved?

Everyone has certain things that make them feel loved. You for instance, if you think back, will remember the moments in your life when you felt especially loved. Think about those times. At that particular moment that you felt loved, was it something the man said to you, was it the way he looked at you or the way you felt when you looked at him, was it something he gave to you, or was it the way he touched you or made love to you?

Just as you have a particular act that makes you feel loved, so does the man you're interested in. All you have to do to push his "love button" is to discover what's made him feel loved in the past. Feeling loved is a pattern we develop. The ways in which we feel love don't change. If certain things made him feel loved once, they will again. Once you've discovered what generated a loving feeling for him in the past, you can replicate it, and he will feel love in the present and for you. Here's how it works.

Let's say you've been interested in a particular man you know well, but only as friends. You spend lots of time together, but you don't seem to be able to get him to see you as a romantic interest. It's often because you're pushing the wrong buttons.

Often when we try to make someone love us, we do what makes *us* feel love. We send good vibes his way or look at him in a certain way, thinking that if he did the same thing to us we'd melt. Or we cook and clean and bake and give gifts, because we've been told that this is the way to make a man fall in love. Only he doesn't feel love because what you're doing is your turnon, not his.

So how do you find out what turns a man on? Ask him questions about the times he's been in love before. Don't be stopped by feeling jealous or competitive when he talks about other women he's loved. After all, he's here, with you, not there in that other time with her. So feel superior instead. You have him, she doesn't.

Let's say you're having a casual lunch with a male friend whom you'd like to turn into a lover, but you don't know how. The first thing you'd want to do is be sure he's available. Next, is he open to commitment? Is he interested in marriage? If you're already friends, these things are easy to find out just by chitchatting about what's happening in his life.

After that, start asking questions about his former loves. For instance, you might ask, "Have you ever been head-over-heels in love?" An innocent enough question.

If he says yes, the next question is easy, "What did you love about her?" Just get him talking about her, and in the act of telling, a funny thing will happen. Because he is remembering the love he once felt for this other woman while he is looking at you, you will be able to take advantage of something called *transference*. He will begin to transfer the feelings he had for her to you.

Then say, "I've been trying to figure out what made me fall for some of the guys in my life. How was it with you and ...? What made you fall? Was it some specific thing she did? Or the situation? Or both?" He'll tell you what she did, and you'll know the key to making him feel loved.

Remember, you are really not in competition with the women

in his past. He has already decided that they're not for him. If you're in competition with anyone, it's the women in his present. What's he thinking about them?

Understanding How He Decides

You can negotiate a relationship without driving yourself crazy if you understand your new man's decision-making process. Study this man you're interested in.

Is he impulsive? If he makes impulsive decisions, then he could suddenly decide he loves you, without a long courtship.

Is he the kind of guy who knows exactly what he wants and then goes after it? Then he may have already decided you're what he wants before he started to date you.

Or is he more thoughtful, a ponderer, someone who studies every side of an issue before making a decision? In this case, no matter how much he cares about you, he's not going to rush into anything.

Does he make decisions by comparing? If so, even if you and he get along like magic, he's going to go out and date other women, just for the sake of comparisons, so he'll know for sure.

Or most dangerously, is he the type that makes an instant decision and then afterward goes around making comparisons to be sure he got a good deal? If so, he may commit to you and *then* have to check around.

Knowing a man's a ponderer won't make you any happier about his taking his sweet time deciding whether he really wants you and seeing other women to make comparisons. But it will make you understand what's going on and not blame yourself. One of the worst mistakes is to start changing yourself or acting desperate because the man you care about is going through his normal decision-making process.

There are always lots of clues about a man's decision-making process—the way he orders dinner, for example. Does he study the whole menu and then order, or does he know exactly what he wants to eat before he even gets to the restaurant? Or does he order and then decide he wants yours instead? Or wish he'd gotten something else? Does he demand that you only go to restaurants he likes?

Handling Men Who Demand Too Much

Men can make all sorts of excessive demands on you—more homemaking than you want to give, kinkier sex than you want to participate in—the demand is too much if it involves a sacrifice you don't feel comfortable making.

Sometimes, you can be unaware that the man is demanding more than you feel comfortable giving. Instead, you may have a feeling of being suffocated. Or, you may suddenly find yourself making up excuses to spend time away from him. Or, you suddenly find yourself harassed, overworked and overscheduled. You just don't have time to pick up the cleaning, drop off the film, call the travel agent and get the VCR fixed.

These are danger signals that the man in your life is demanding too much.

If you've already given in more than you should, if you're already doing more than you want to do, you're soon going to resent the man in your life. The relationship is already in trouble, and the solution is to sit down with him and let him know that his demands are excessive and that you absolutely, positively aren't going to continue giving in.

The longer you've been giving in, the more difficult it becomes to stop. He's used to having you bend to his will. And now you don't want to do it anymore. Don't be surprised if he gets angry, feels betrayed and leaves. The good news is he'll probably be back. And when he does come back, start fresh. Refuse to do anything that will make you feel used. Start negotiating some of those responsibilities back onto his list.

Having Space for a Man

A man wants to feel welcome in your life. Some women's physical surroundings don't show much of a welcome mat.

Eleanor had no trouble attracting men. She wore a mane of wild-looking, waist-length auburn hair. Her blue eyes were outlined with brown lashes, and she dressed in bright colors and always looked interesting and erotic.

As an interior decorator for large office buildings, she had a booming business and a big staff. She was a member of a computer dating service, but was having trouble meeting a man who wanted a real relationship with her. They all met her, took her out a few times, had sex with her and left. "Am I just a lousy lay or what?" she complained to me as we tried to analyze her problem.

By happenstance, I knew one of the men who had briefly dated Eleanor. She begged me to call him to get the male side of the story.

"She has this wanton woman look," he told me, "but when you get to know her, she's not like that at all.

"Take her house. It's beautiful, but it's sure not sexy—all art deco, pink and black with white rugs and silver furniture. Huge fake flower arrangements in big black jars. Not a comfortable chair or a place to put a drink down in the whole house. Just too perfect. You don't even want to step on the white rug. Only an interior decorator could be happy there."

An interesting comment, in view of Eleanor's taste in men. "I seem to spend most of my time with gay decorators, and some have become good friends," she explained to me, "but what I'm looking for in a husband is a real he-man."

I had to explain to Eleanor that as long as she treated her home as a decorator showroom, it would act as a major turnoff for precisely the kind of men she desired. Eleanor, fiercely proud of her decorating skills, stood on principle. Her home was her castle. The right man would appreciate both her and her home. When I last heard from her, she still hadn't found a man.

While Eleanor's space was so perfect it was off-putting for most men, a woman's living style can keep a man from getting closer for the opposite reason. Nancy, a social worker, never seemed to have time to straighten her apartment. "It's getting worse and worse. I can't even let a man in the bedroom area. I'd be too embarrassed," she said.

Naturally, Nancy's mess never stayed hidden from men for long. They came, they saw, they left. She was unwilling or unable to change her habits, and nobody was willing to take the plunge and actually try to live with her. Her friends had almost convinced her that no man would ever love her because she was so messy. On the other hand, Nancy was warm, giving and easy to be with. She finally got lucky.

When she met Ed, they liked each other right away. "I've always been an organizer, and I had this strong feeling that I could help her arrange things," he admitted after they'd been married for two years. "I know some guys just assume that keeping things in order is a woman's job. Well, that's not what Nancy's good at, so when we moved, I got her stuff halfway sorted when we packed her up, and then really organized in our new house. She's still not neat, but we're doing fine."

What is it that your house or apartment says about you? Is it a study in perfection like Eleanor's, a mess like Nancy's, or is it inviting to a man? Does it show him that he'd have a comfortable place in a home you shared together?

CHAPTER TWELVE

The "One True Love" Myth

At first I was totally mystified by a group of strikingly attractive women who seemed to find love, only to have it slip through their grasp—over and over again. Each relationship would last from six weeks to two years and then self-destruct. Lots of men passed through their lives, and after a series of these relationships, they were suddenly thirty-five years old with no one to love.

Finally, I realized that they were all tragically caught up in a persistent myth: That for every woman, there is just one man in all the world who is her "one true love." Each of these women was convinced that she had already met and lost her "one true love." From then on, all her subsequent relationships were doomed.

In one way or another, consciously or unconsciously, these women worked to preserve the "one true love" myth, even while destroying their chances of finding real love. Sometimes, out of a misplaced feeling of loyalty to their one true love, they held back from others. In other cases, they plunged into a new relationship, but without any real hope that it would last, because they *knew* they had already had the best love ever. Their expectation that love wouldn't last became a self-fulfilling prophecy.

Through marriages and divorces, relationships with jerks and with nice guys, they waited for their one true love to return.

Cindy, a petite thirty-six-year-old brunette, was working as a soap opera costume lady in Hollywood when she came to me.

"I'm so unhappy. My marriage was a mistake," she told me, "and all my relationships since then haven't worked either. I don't know what's wrong with me.

"I was only nineteen when I married Marco in 1970. Marco was a macho Italian man. We lived together in Boston, where I was going to school. Those were the hippie days, and I wanted exactly the opposite of my family. I was rebelling against their values, and maybe that's why I married Marco. His Italian background was so different. He wasn't religious at all, a change from my religious Jewish family.

"We had a big wedding, but I somehow knew when I took those vows that we wouldn't stay married. Sex was about the only thing holding us together. We fought a lot, but I didn't really know anything about men or relationships, so I didn't know how two people were supposed to act together.

"Then after we were married a year and a half, I found out he was using drugs. I couldn't believe it at first, but the evidence was overwhelming. My girlfriend and I were rearranging his shoes in the closet when I found a bunch of syringes in his shoe. My friend and I cut them into little pieces, and when he came in, I threw them at him. 'Here, put this in your veins,' I screamed. 'Shoot up with this if you can.'

"I was so naive, I never suspected anything. I since found out that my brother and all my friends were taking drugs with him. He's just disappeared from my life. He could be dead for all I know. I heard from him once, on September 17, about ten years ago. He called and said 'Happy Birthday,' and I said, 'You know my birthday is November 17, not September 17.'

"I had a restraining order that he couldn't come within five miles of my house, but he found me and called anyway. 'You know it's not my birthday,' I accused him.

" 'I want my clothes,' he said, and I said, 'You'll get your clothes when I get my albums.' It sounds so childish now."

Cindy had inherited an erroneous belief system about the length of relationships from her mother. "My mother married four times, the first two times for only six months each, so I guess I thought it was okay to get out fast if it didn't work.

"Then she married my father, and they were together twelve years before he died in a boating accident. He was twenty-one years older, and she said he was her prince, her rock of Gibralter, her security, and he gave her a future she never had. Then she married my stepfather, and they've been married for twenty-seven years now."

Cindy kept saying things like, "A relationship is a lot of work. I'm too independent. I haven't found anyone worth going through that for." But her real problem was a love that got away.

"After I left Marco," she went on, "I met the man of my dreams, Jean-Pierre. He was a gorgeous, wonderful Frenchman. I met him in Miami when I was getting my divorce from Marco. He was from Montreal. He looked like a picture of Jesus Christ, with long hair, blue eyes and a dark beard. We fell madly in love."

Young, Idyllic Love

"I followed him to Montreal and went to school there, and we lived together. We were happy, but I started having stupid second thoughts, worrying that I was making the same mistake again, that maybe I should look for someone whose background was more similar to mine.

"So when I graduated from school that year, I took a job in D.C. It wasn't that great a job. Maybe I was trying to test my relationship with Jean-Pierre. But he was good about coming down to visit me.

"Then it happened. He was two days late coming down from Montreal, it was a Saturday, and I was bored. So I made a date and went out with this doctor I'd met. Our date was for lunch, but I was having a good time and we wound up going to an exhibit of King Tut. Meanwhile, Jean-Pierre had gotten in, not found me at home and decided to kill some time. I'll never forget it. We walked out of the exhibit hall, arm in arm, and there's my Frenchman, standing in line.

"He saw us, and that was the end of that. I don't know why I didn't just run over to him. I certainly didn't care anything about the doctor. I guess I was flustered, and ashamed maybe. Anyway, I never saw Jean-Pierre or heard from him again. I've lamented that day for many, many years. He was so perfect for me. I loved him and he loved me."

When You Don't Know What's Happened to Him

"I tried for years to get back in touch with him. I even found an old phone book and as recently as 1981 I made a lot of phone calls to Montreal to try to locate him. Unfortunately, he has a very common French name.

"I guess I have this great unrequited love that I've never gotten over. I've always regretted that day, and I guess one thing that keeps me from getting close to other men is because I feel I have this unfinished business in my life with this other man. What can I do?"

It was apparent that Cindy would have to close that chapter of her life. If she couldn't forget Jean-Pierre, maybe she could try to satisfy herself that he could either be found or was truly gone forever. When I suggested this to Cindy, she became misty. The very thought released emotions that she had held in check for many years.

Cindy felt helpless about tracking down Jean-Pierre, although she really wasn't. Just as she would hire an expert to do anything else she needed done, I suggested she find an expert to help her. After all, she wouldn't try to find a house to buy without a realtor to help, so why look for a missing person alone? Cindy decided to contact a "finder of lost loves."

She found one listed under "detectives" in the L.A. phone book, as well as two ads for other "finders" in the classified ads in the L.A. *Times*. The amounts for a search started at $99.

Cindy's assignment for the week was to write a letter to Jean-

Pierre, explaining how badly she's felt for all these years and asking him if he'd possibly consider a meeting or a conversation with her.

Releasing Your Feelings

Just writing down all the guilt and anguish she'd been carrying around all those years was a release. Having put the words on paper, she didn't have the weight of them in her heart.

Then she was to contact a "finder of lost loves" and get started. The finder would deliver her letter, should he be able to find Jean-Pierre. In all, for no more than the cost of a fancy dinner out, she could feel good about having done as much as she could.

"I can't believe how good it feels to put this problem in someone else's hands," she reported afterward. "I'm so relieved."

It took only two weeks for the "finder of lost loves" to find Cindy's old flame and deliver her letter. Jean-Pierre called her, and they had a long talk.

"He's married, with three sons." Cindy reported to me. "He's very proud of them and kept telling me about them. He was about to leave on a fishing trip with the two older boys. He sounds very devoted to his wife, too. Kept saying how he'd like me to meet his family. He didn't say much about the letter, except that I didn't need to apologize, it was all so long ago. He sounded different than I remembered—real domestic, not very sophisticated.

"I guess I should feel totally crushed. I mean, there's no way we could get back together again. Actually, what I feel worst about is that he went on with his life and I didn't. Now I've got to rush to catch up. Why do I feel relieved? Maybe because I hate fishing. Oh, I'm all mixed up. I should be in mourning, for God's sake."

I told Cindy to sleep on it, that everything was going to be fine. Later, more settled down, she told me, "I felt as if someone pulled a plug that was holding back my emotions," she told me. "I know I've been witholding from men. I was just so full of unspoken words and feelings for Jean-Pierre. Now maybe I can give up carrying a torch and be free to start again."

If you have a pattern like Cindy's where your relationships don't last longer than two years, look at the reasons why.

The Two-Year Limit

One cause of relationships not lasting more than two years is that the "in love" feeling usually only lasts from six months to two years. After that period, reality sets in, problems come up and we begin to see faults in the other person. If the relationship is sound, though, we begin to bond in a deeper, more spiritual, more permanent manner. If you're already bonded to someone else psychologically, the relationship can't make that transition, so you move on in search of new "in love" feelings.

There's nothing wrong with remembering an old love fondly. After all, you shared lots of memories. But when the memories become overpowering, they can keep you from falling in love again.

Your "one true love" is always unsatisfying in one great way. Usually it's because he's gone, like Jean-Pierre. Or even worse, he's there, you can still see him, but you can't have him. Yet, because you believe he's your "one true love," you feel you're being unfaithful if you let anyone else come close.

Vivian was trapped in this kind of "one true love" relationship for fifteen years, keeping her from finding real love. A thirty-nine-year-old talk show producer, Vivian grew up as the only girl in a family of six boys, all but one of whom was older than she.

"I was a tomboy," she said, white teeth flashing a quick smile like bright pearls against her almond skin. "I was the center of my brothers' universe. They doted on me and gave me everything. I grew up with a very healthy view of how men liked me, even adored me, just for being me.

"I met Mel at a Jesse Jackson Operation Push meeting. He was in the record promotion business. In the beginning, I wasn't too impressed. He'd make a date, and if business came up, he'd cancel.

"By 1974 we were going out a lot. Seeing him taking care of business, in control and decisive, was a turnon for me. He wasn't the handsomest, best-educated man I'd ever dated, but he was a take-charge kind of person.

"The record business can be very glamorous—payola, unlimited expense accounts and parties every night. He was thirty-five and I was in my twenties. But there was more than the glamor. He took care of me. I loved the way he supported me. He told me I could do more; he encouraged me to be my best self. He was my cheerleader and coach. He'd say, 'Do this and say this and you'll get promoted.' And I did and it would work, and I began to respect him even more.

"But we had constant fights. Over lots of things, but mostly about him not showing for a date and not even calling. I'd be furious, and then he'd come back with apologies and presents.

"We were hooked into an endless series of fights and passionate reconciliations afterwards. Asking for forgiveness was an art with him. I would be so angry. I remember I called him one time and I said, 'You son of a bitch. I hate you. I'm so tired of this bullshit. I can't take this anymore. I never want to see you again,' and he said, 'Just let me put you on hold for one sec. I really want to talk to you, but I'm on another call,' and he put me on hold.

"Then when he came back on the line he said, 'I am so hungry. I'm starving to death. Will you go to dinner with me? You know how I hate to eat alone.'

"I was at home dressing and crying at the same time. I was so upset with myself. Yet there I was, going back to him again. When I got in the car, I was so mad I couldn't talk to him, but we went to dinner and by the end of the evening I'd forgiven him again.

"We had been together for two years when I said, 'I've had enough.' We broke up, and I was physically ill. I'd come home from work and go right to bed, where I'd stay and cry myself to sleep. After about three weeks, I started coming around, and I thought, 'Well, I'm starting to get myself under control.' "

Can't Get Away from Him

"Three or four months later, I decided to call him and just be friends. 'After all,' I thought, 'why can't we just be friends?' Professionally, he was the best counselor I ever had. I called him.

"A woman answered the phone. I asked for him. He came to

the phone and said, 'I'll meet you somewhere.' He came and took me to dinner and told me that this woman, Tawny, was living with him. I was devastated. I began to cry in the restaurant. I couldn't help myself.

"I didn't know how much I still cared about him until then. When I fell apart in the restaurant, the whole display turned him on. He got hooked on me again, and we had a torrid affair while he was living with Tawny. I asked him to leave her, and he said he couldn't.

"Then I met Ross, and a few months later he moved in with me. Mel's with Tawny. I'm with Ross. I ran into Mel at a party and told him I'm living with someone, and he went berserk. He started calling me, and he said, 'You know I love you. Don't do this.'

"Ross wanted to get married. I had two young kids from a previous marriage, so I married him. He was gorgeous, an ex-football player and a financial planner. Just before I got married, Mel called and said, 'Don't marry him. You aren't in love with him.'

"Ross started acting like a jerk as soon as I married him. He was used to a flamboyant life. He was right off the cover of *Gentlemen's Quarterly*. The whole world was after him, and people couldn't believe he'd married a woman with two kids.

"He couldn't give up the fast life. He wanted to have his cake and eat it too. He wanted a family, and he wanted to do whatever he wanted to do whenever he wanted to do it. Through all this, Mel called constantly.

"I was back in Chicago and my marriage was falling apart. Mel would call and tell me what to do. He was emotionally supportive. We started seeing each other again on the sly, and the sex was still terrific.

"Tawny had to know about me because I would call Mel and she would answer the phone. Once we were supposed to fly out to the coast together. He was supposed to meet me at the airport, and he never showed up. No phone call, no message, no nothing. So I went out to California all by myself. I called Tawny and asked if he was there. She said no. I said, 'You tell that son of a bitch he can kiss my ass.' She sure had to suspect something.

"The next day he showed up where I was staying in California.

He said he came to break up, and of course, it turned into another torrid weekend.

"After my divorce from Ross, I was on a business trip to the coast and again ran into Mel. I asked him to leave Tawny, and he wouldn't. I went back to Chicago and figured it was over.

"A year later, I got an invitation to an Earth Wind and Fire party, and I thought he'd be there. 'I'm a big girl,' I thought. 'I'll go to the party. It'll be good for me.' So I got to the party and he wasn't there. I was relieved, and then on the way out the door, there he was, right in my face. I thought to myself, 'I can handle this.'

" 'How are you?' he asked, and I said, 'Fine, how are you?' And he said, 'Did you recover from your divorce?' And I said, 'Almost.' And he said, 'I know how it is. Tawny and I are separated. I'm recovering too.'

"Then he put his hotel key in my hand like a scene from a bad movie.

" 'If you don't come, I'll understand,' he whispered. Of course, I took the key, thinking to myself, 'You dummy,' but I couldn't help myself. I went to his room, and the whole crazy thing started over again. Only this time it was different. We were both free. It was 1984. I was living in Chicago and he was living in L.A.

"I gave him an ultimatum. 'If you don't ask me to marry you in a year, forget it.' The year went by, but meanwhile, I started dating this younger guy who treated me great. So when the day came and the year was up and he said he wasn't ready yet, I told myself it was okay because I had the best of both worlds. I could go to L.A. and sit by the pool with Mel and then come back and be wined and dined by a younger man in Chicago.

"A few months later I had to move to New York for work, but I didn't really like it there. Soon after, Mel called and said, 'Get on the plane. Don't think about it. Just do it. I'm ready.'

"I said I couldn't just do it. I needed to plan, to wind up my commitments in New York. I'd already been thinking that I could do more in the television field in L.A., and I thought that if I was in L.A., Mel and I could have a normal relationship, get engaged in a normal way and get married. So I told him I needed about two months. He didn't call much over the next few weeks, but I figured he was still angry because I wouldn't just drop everything and come when he said to.

"Six weeks later, when I called Mel to let him know my flight plans, he said he was going to get married to a woman he'd been dating out in L.A. I was stunned, but because he was only about one-third the reason I wanted to move to L.A., I moved anyway. It was 1988.

"After I got there, it started out with me thinking to myself, 'Why can't we just be friends, even if he's married? We've meant so much to each other, and he's helped me so much.'

"He kept telling me it's okay, we can just be friends. He would come and pick me up and take me to lunch. One day, I was still getting ready, and when I came out of the bedroom, he didn't have any clothes on. We started up again hot, and it faded away and then it torched up again when I was buying my house. I had fallen into the habit of calling him whenever I needed help. I depended on him like I used to depend on my brothers to take care of me.

"I called him for advice on buying my house. He's in his element when I need him, and this was a major project. He got all the paperwork done, helped me with money, moved me in, bought my appliances and drapes. I was seeing him almost every day. By then, though, I knew what was going on. I told him, 'You're back in my life, calling three times a day and then you're going to split.'

"Of course, that's exactly what he did. After I moved into the house, he vanished. All this attention, then suddenly no calls for two weeks, like he'd dropped off the face of the earth. I called his office and his partner said, 'He's away on vacation, didn't you know?'

"When he finally called me I was furious. 'How could you just go away and not even tell me you're going? It's only common courtesy after seeing each other almost every day and you calling all the time.'

" 'I don't have to tell you where I'm going,' he said, 'and I knew you'd be upset if I told you I took my wife to Paris.'

" 'I respect the limits of our relationship,' " I shot back at him. " 'I know you can take your wife away where you can't take me, but I do have the right to know. You should have told me.'

" 'I don't have to tell you anything. You don't love me.'

" 'You son of a bitch. You rotten bastard. You can't tell me I don't love you.' I screamed into the phone.

" 'I don't have to talk to you.' He hung up.

"I didn't talk to him again until I saw him at a party at Christmas and he said, 'You look so good. You made me so mad the last time we fought, I ripped your page out of my book and threw it away. Can I have your number? Just to keep up. As friends.'

"I told him no.

" 'I don't blame you,' he said. 'I'm sorry.'

"The other night I had a dream about him. I dreamed he said, 'I'm leaving my wife and I want to marry you.' "

At the time Vivian related her story to me, it had been almost a year since she'd been intimate with Mel. I explained to her that her "one true love" problem was only in remission. Like a recovered alcoholic who always remains just one drink away from runaway alcoholism, she can't see Mel or talk to him even once or she risks his dominating her life again.

Vivian's perspective on the situation is improving the longer she's away from Mel. She's beginning to realize that she and Mel can only exist as a couple in trauma. Their relationship is based on passion, on anger, on the kind of love that only leads to breaking up and making up, but not lifelong love.

I have never known a couple with this kind of stormy relationship to become happy together. The drama and conflict just escalate, and the woman's self-esteem steadily erodes. Each time Vivian takes Mel back she winds up with the same problems, and she begins to hate herself for being so stupid.

While Vivian understands this, Mel still haunts her thoughts. The intensity of the passion they shared together and Vivian's need for the kind of support Mel provided made Mel seem to be the love of her life—one that can never be equaled. It will be hard for Vivian to overcome these thoughts and open her mind to the possibility of another man offering her more.

As she gets further away from Mel, though, Vivian finds that she is gradually beginning to get closer to other men. She's also beginning to face the fact that no one man is ever going to give her the adoration she got from her brothers.

Vivian and Cindy are not the only examples of women wasting their lives on an unrequited fantasy "true love" that they'll never get. In their cases, they were carrying a torch for someone they actually had a relationship with. Sometimes, the "one true love" can be someone with whom you've never had a romance and never could. Such was the case with Kimberly.

Still In Love with Daddy

Kimberly's feelings for her father had always stood in the way of deeper bonding with a man. When Kimberly came to me, she was filled with guilt and remorse for all the good ones she'd let get away after a brief romance. Losing Jay hurt the most.

"Before I moved to L.A., I lived with Jay for two years," Kimberly related when she first came to see me.

"I kept in touch with Jay after that, and we stayed friends. I introduced him to my best friend, Sue, and they were married for five years and then they divorced. Right after they'd divorced, Jay was in a car accident, and Sue asked me if I'd check up on him in the hospital since she had moved to New York.

"I began to visit him, and we just sort of fell in love all over again. At that point I was between relationships. When he got out of the hospital, he came and stayed with me to recuperate. Well, soon we were in bed together. The sex was as great as ever. He was a musician, and when he recovered, he got a job with a music publisher.

"Everything should have been perfect, but deep down, I still thought he wasn't good enough. It seems that nobody is ever good enough for me. He was so wonderful, and yet I'm never satisfied. I'm always looking for a father substitute, and nobody ever lives up to my father. Daddy died when I was sixteen, and he was the best person on earth.

"I guess I'm afraid if I get too close to a man he'll leave me like my father did," she said, giving me the pat explanation she'd always given.

But I thought there was more. When I suggested that loving a man and making a permanent commitment might seem to be a betrayal of the memory of her father's great love, she began to cry. It was true. As long as the memory of her father held the place of first man in her life, she couldn't give that spot to someone else. And Kimberly also couldn't stop comparing every man she met with her father.

"I had just sold my dress shop and was going to work for Saks as a buyer. Jay and I had a good life, but I decided that Jay just wasn't doing it for me financially. I know it sounds horrible, but that's how I felt at the time. The house I grew up in is now an embassy. I guess I always thought that the man I fell in love with would put me in a castle like Daddy did.

" 'This isn't working for me' I announced to Jay one day. I can be really hard—it's my shell, my way of dealing with relationships when I want out. I know Jay was heartbroken, and now I'm sorry.

"I'd settle for other things now. I don't need a man to give me a castle anymore, just a lot of love will do. Jay isn't rich, but he's well off enough for most women. I wish I had him back."

I first saw Kimberly in March. We were making progress on normalizing her relationships with men when fate threw her and Jay together.

This time, Kimberly didn't turn down what Jay had to offer. Instead, she gratefully accepted the love he had to give and was able to return his love as well.

"I finally realized I need a real man, not a memory, and my love for Jay has nothing to do with the memory of my father."

Any woman over thirty who can't stay in a relationship because no one ever seems to compare to a lost love or who spends years yearning for a man she never gets may be trapped in the "one true love" myth. If this describes your situation, you're in danger of wasting your life and should get some counseling, if for nothing more than a quick reality check.

CHAPTER THIRTEEN

Compromises and Trade-Offs

"I'm not going to settle!" Rebecca was angry at the very idea that she wouldn't get everything she wanted in a man. Her brown eyes blazed with anger. Her chin jutted forward. "I still want children. It's not too late. My body's in great shape. But I don't want to be a single mother. I want a man who makes very good money and who will be a good father."

At forty, Rebecca's dating options seemed to be closing in. The men she met who were rich enough for her were too old to make good fathers in her opinion. Or they had already had families and didn't want to start another one. The men who were young enough to start a family with Rebecca didn't have enough money.

I explained to Rebecca that she could have any one thing she wanted, but she would never get everything, especially not all at once. You can be a devoted mother or a hard-driving CEO, but it's nearly impossible to be both at the same time. Babies still aren't welcome in the boardrooms of America.

We women are willing to make compromises in almost every area of life, yet we go crazy at the suggestion that we might have to make some compromises where love is concerned. In fact, this is another failure pattern.

Failure Pattern 6: Inability to Compromise

When you buy a house, you compromise. You buy the big house in the not-so-terrific neighborhood or you buy the little house in the great neighborhood. You give up a huge lot for a view, RV parking for a swimming pool. We accept this.

But when it comes to finding love, we all want our fantasies fulfilled. So we begin to compare the men we meet with some movie star image or some fantasy ideal of perfection instead of to other real men.

The Myth of the Perfect Man

The myth of "the perfect man" is very similar to the "one true love" myth, and it causes just as much misery. Many women evidently took Mom literally when she said, "There'll be someone out there, dear, who will be just perfect for you." They spend their lives pursuing the mythical "perfect man" like a quest for the Holy Grail.

If the terrific guy they have shows an imperfection that bothers them, this *proves* he's not the right man for them. So they move on and keep looking, because somewhere in the world is their "perfect man."

These women will acknowledge that no man is really perfect. And then they add, "But you don't understand. He doesn't have to be perfect. He just has to be perfect for me."

No one is perfect, even for another person. The "perfect man" myth is a myth no matter how it's stated. And there are no perfect marriages. There are only two people who love each other and live with each other's imperfections.

Some couples do seem to mesh better than others, but you can never know how much they each had to compromise and how much give and take was involved to make their "fit" look so perfect from the outside.

Even couples with serious problems often maintain the pretense of happiness right up until they file for divorce. It's all too easy when you're single to look at someone else's marriage and think, "She has a perfect marriage. She has a perfect husband, a perfect house, perfect kids and a perfect life. That's what I want." But don't be fooled. If you were to step into her shoes, you might find that her husband has a floozy on the side and hasn't had sex with her in eight months, that the kids are dealing drugs and that she looks so content because she's on Valium twenty-four hours a day!

Unfortunately, when we first fall in love, we really don't *want* to see anything wrong with the love object. We want to believe that he's truly perfect, so we blind ourselves to his flaws. Sometimes we don't wake up to them and face them until later, after we've invested months in a relationship.

The key to building a relationship on a realistic basis is to give up the "perfect man" myth and *expect* flaws. Try to find out about a man's imperfections as quickly as possible, *before* you're head-over-heels in love and too far gone to decide rationally if you can live with them.

One reason it's important to find out what's wrong with a man as soon as possible is that whatever bothers you during the beginning of a relationship only gets worse. I found this out some years ago when I fell in love with a prominent psychiatrist.

The sex was great. His company was wonderful. We had so much in common. He was perfect, except that he had one little flaw. He hummed all the time. Not a loud hum, just barely audible, like old men praying in the synagogue, the words discernible only to him, running together like a record played at fast speed.

At first I thought, "Such a small thing. Hardly anyone else notices. I can overlook it. It only annoys me a little bit." But as the weeks wore on and we got closer and started to spend more and more time together, the humming began to drive me crazy.

"Can't you stop that incessant humming," I'd ask him. "What, I was humming?" He'd reply. It was so habitual he wasn't even aware he was doing it.

I suppose if I'd really been crazy in love with him, I would have hummed along to be more in tune. But even then, it might not have been a great idea. I too could have become an incessant hummer.

If you think about it, you probably have some annoying habits too. After five years of being married and constantly loved, I had almost forgotten my own imperfections until I happened to speak to an ex-boyfriend. I had called him to see if he'd appear on the "Donahue Show" for my friend's book, *Men Who Can't Be Faithful*, so you know the kind of guy he was.

"Are you and your husband still faithful?" he wanted to know. "Of course," I told him. "We love each other."

Then, still as wonderful as ever, he said, "I can't understand why your husband loves you so much. I lived with you. I know what you're like. You can't cook. You pile your clothes and papers up all over the house. You don't keep house. What on earth does he see in you?"

"Luckily, more than you did," I thought.

We all have some not so great qualities that come along with our good ones. We are all a package deal. The man who marries you will have to live with your bad traits as well as your good ones. And you will have to live with his bad traits too.

Finding His Flaws

Some men are clever at disguising their mean, insensitive, dishonest side when they meet you and when they're courting. But they can't hide it forever, and there are early warning signs when a man isn't as great as he appears. If he doesn't have lots of long-time friends, you should wonder why. It could be because he's not a good friend. If his ex-wife/girlfriend doesn't speak to him, it's probably because he's done something unspeakable.

Sheila, a tall redhead with big blue eyes and long dark lashes, used to be a model and was now working as a writer on a Hollywood sitcom. When she came to see me, she was in a relationship with a married studio head, a much older man.

He didn't seem to have any close friends, a definite warning sign, but Sheila didn't care. At thirty-one, she had already been divorced twice. Her second husband was a lawyer who had moved into her house, lived there during their marriage and then claimed half the house in the divorce. She had been forced to buy half her own house back from him and was very cynical about men and relationships.

"I've already been burned twice," she told me. "But my relationship with Howard is perfect. He's rich, and he seems crazy about me. He buys me presents and takes me on wonderful trips to Las Vegas where we stay in these incredible suites. His reputation at the studio is really lousy, though—everyone's afraid of him, no one likes him, and I've heard that he treats his wife terribly. But he's been nice to me. He helps me with my career.

"The problem is, I recently met a nice guy about my own age, Malcolm. He sells computer chips or something for computers. Anyway, we've started seeing each other.

"I know Howard's going to be upset if he finds out about Malcolm. And he can be mean when he gets mad. But I'm getting to like Malcolm a lot. He's young, strong, a great lover and a handyman to boot—he fixes things around my house.

"The trouble with Malcolm is that I wouldn't have any security. He's not poor, but he certainly doesn't have Howard's money. But Malcolm's the kind of man I could really get serious about and marry, and I worry about getting into another bad marriage, so maybe I should forget Malcolm and stick with Howard. What should I do?"

Sheila's was not an unusual problem. Often a woman is so afraid of a bad marriage that she'll ignore a man's flaws and stay in an ultimately unfulfilling relationship, or even in a bad relationship, just to avoid the risk of failing at marriage.

I suspected what the outcome was going to be, but it was important for Sheila to make her own choice between the two men in her life, so I advised her to continue seeing both until the choice became obvious.

As she was becoming closer to Malcolm, her older lover found out that she had another man in her life. Instead of making trouble for Malcolm, though, as Sheila had feared, Howard caved in under the stress of competition.

"He's calling me and pleading with me to see him," she reported. "He keeps begging me to stop seeing Malcolm."

Sheila was nearing a choice. Suddenly, Howard's flaws were apparent to her. He was no longer the wonderful older man she looked up to, the powerful man who rented private jets and stayed in fancy suites. He was old, frail, insecure, whiny and an annoyance. It didn't take long for Sheila to choose Malcolm, even if he wasn't rich.

If Howard hadn't been married, Sheila could easily have wound up married to the wrong man and become a rich but badly treated wife. Ignoring a man's flaws because of his money and power is a big mistake. He could lose his money and his power and you'd be stuck with what's left.

Sure, men can change. Even Howard might have become sweet in his dotage. Fat men become thin. Slobs become neat. Drug addicts stop using drugs. Abusers sometimes become loving. Drunks become nondrinkers. But only rarely. Such men don't change easily, and they can't be changed by you.

Men Who Won't Change

You can't love a man into changing, and you can't bully him into changing. You can't really do anything about changing the basic character traits a man has. If he's mean, he'll probably stay that way. If he's insensitive, he probably won't become sensitive. If he lies, he won't become honest.

I dated an alcoholic for much longer than I should have. Of course, like many naive women who get involved with alcoholics, I didn't recognize the symptoms in the beginning, and when I finally did, I thought my good influence would help keep him sober.

Lou was a blind date I made and didn't feel like going on when the time came. I had a cold. But he was so engaging on the phone that he made me laugh and convinced me to go out with him anyway. When he arrived at the door, I wished I'd gotten more fixed up.

He was about six feet, two inches tall, with curly black hair, twinkly blue eyes and a good build with a muscular chest and flat tummy. He drove a vintage MG and had his own small television production company, a promising career as a director on a prime-time comedy show, a house in Santa Monica and a fabulous sense of humor. I was particularly impressed that first night because when he got ice cubes from my freezer, he refilled the ice cube trays and carefully put them back.

From the beginning, ice cubes were important. I had stepped into a real-life version of the "Days of Wine and Roses" without realizing it. Lou would make us wonderful frozen drinks, and we'd drive in his little MG to screenings of new movies. I even got to play a part in a commercial he made. I had no way of knowing, but his career was already starting downhill.

Even though he usually went through a whole bottle of liquor in an evening, I didn't face the fact that he had a serious drinking problem until he took me camping in Death Valley to see the wildflowers bloom in the spring. It would be my first time camping, even in a camper. An adventure. And at first, it *was* wonderful. He was so sweet. We hiked to a waterfall and took pictures of the wildflowers. He had even remembered to bring carrots to feed to the wild burros. We visited Scotty's Castle and then had a fancy dinner at the only resort in Death Valley, the Furnace Creek Inn.

Meanwhile, Lou had been drinking steadily and was getting louder and louder. We danced, a bit unsteadily on his part, after dinner at the inn.

By the end of the evening, Lou was lying on the beautiful green lawn in front of the resort, crying. I coaxed him into the camper, drunk and obscene, and I slept on the roof to get away from his smell, his rantings and his burps.

By morning, he was still awake and, unbelievably, more drunk than ever. I suddenly realized that he must have had more bottles stashed in the camper. Disgusted, I drove the camper back to L.A., straight through, trying to ignore this indignant, foul-smelling monster in the back. Every time we passed a truck and the camper swayed, Lou would start cursing and belching. I swore a thousand times over I'd never see him again.

But when he was sober, he was oh so sweet. He'd give you the shirt off his back. He was always there to fix my fence, feed my dog when I was away, help me get a job, solder my stereo wires together or anything else I might need. He was generous, kind and a lot of fun until he got drunk. He'd cook for me. But he'd always plead, "Stop on your way over and buy me a bottle of vodka, please. I haven't had a drink all day and there's nothing in the house." I'd bring the bottle, never realizing that it could have been his third or fourth.

"I need to drink," he rationalized. "I'm funny when I drink. People like me more when I'm drunk."

"You're not funnier. You're stupid and obnoxious, and you repeat yourself. Only other drunks like you," I screamed back. He was so frustrating.

One time Lou got drunk with a friend's husband at a party at her house. When he fell down in the front hallway and wouldn't get up, I had had it. Instead of cajoling and begging and dragging him to the car, I just went home alone. The next day he was really upset. "How could you leave me there?" he wanted to know. Drunks always trust that someone (you) will take care of them.

In spite of my promises to myself, I took him back over and over, and he always got drunk. Meanwhile, his life started to fall apart. Business was bad. He sold the house and moved into a singles' complex.

Soon, nobody in Hollywood would hire him. The word was out. "I'll stop drinking when I get to produce this film I want to make. When I get to be a feature film producer," he'd swear. "I'd stop drinking if I got a job." But, of course, he never did.

Finally, even I had to admit he was impossible, and I left him for good. He had one or two relationships after that, but he was on a fast downhill slide. The last time I saw him he was living out of an old station wagon, getting "detoxed" at the veteran's center and talking about having a liver operation in the near future. I should have been sympathetic, but instead, I was angry. How could he do this to himself? To the wonderful person I once dated?

Why Changing a Man Is Dangerous

While you can't change a man, a man can change himself—but only if he is highly motivated and really works at it for a long time.

There's always the danger that when a man changes, the "new" man will want a new woman, so think twice before you collaborate on such a project.

When Gail met Kelly, she told me, "This is it. I'm going to marry him." And she might have, if she hadn't worked so hard to get him to change.

Kelly, a fast-living freelance journalist, had been known as one of the biggest players in town when he and Gail got together. He had been a bon vivant, with a new woman on his arm all the time, and a gourmand, eating everything in sight and smoking a cigar afterwards. Kelly's sardonic wit and "live for today" philosophy were the centerpiece of every wild gathering.

Gail, on the other hand, was a poet. She dabbled with freelance writing, but in general thought anything but poetry was beneath her. Many people thought they were the perfect couple. Neither one was very secure, but they seemed to thrive on their bohemian lifestyle.

Almost as soon as they were living together, Gail began trying to get Kelly to change. She no longer liked his freelance friends. She wanted him to get a job, to take care of her.

Kelly caved in to her nagging, shaved his beard, put on a three-piece suit and got a job in a publishing company. "Wait till you see Kelly without his beard, Tracy. And he's so cute in a business suit!" Gail cooed to me, calling in triumph to tell me about Kelly's new job. And indeed he was cute.

Gail kept up the pressure, next urging him to get healthy. She helped him to lose weight and to give up drinking. He started working out and became lean and muscular. Old friends didn't recognize him on the street. He looked like a different person. And he was. . . .

Gail became a cheering section for him. She went around behind him everywhere saying, "Oh, isn't he gorgeous? Isn't he just gorgeous?" Soon all the other women in sight began to notice how gorgeous Kelly was. Soon Kelly began to believe it himself.

So impressive was the "new" Kelly, his employers promoted him to a much higher, better-paying position. No longer the drunken life of the party, he turned his quick wit to social climbing and began to move in tonier, more upscale circles.

Gail's fantasy was fulfilled. Now Kelly went to work every day and she stayed home and took care of him. She cooked for him, she ironed his clothes and she wrote poetry. Gail was still the same. Still bohemian looking, wearing long skirts and peasant blouses, sandals and no makeup. The only problem was that Gail, just moderately attractive, no longer fit Kelly's lifestyle.

He wanted someone taller, someone who dressed better, who was more socially appropriate for his new position in life. Kelly was into money and getting ahead, and he wanted a woman who earned her own way and who contributed financially. He tried getting assignments for Gail, but when they were offered, she either turned them down or never did them.

It was obvious that Gail had gotten Kelly to change, but then refused to change herself. She thought life would be the same, never taking into account Kelly's new yuppie values—the ones she had pushed on him.

Kelly and Gail split up. Less than a year later, Kelly married someone not at all like Gail.

Brokenhearted, Gail saw the mistake she'd made. "I should have let him stay the way he was," she told me angrily after she heard about Kelly's wedding. "I did everything to push him to change. Now he's successful, and he won't even talk to me anymore. The next guy I meet, I'm going to let stay just the way he is. You can bet on it."

Gail couldn't have prevented Kelly from trying to better his career, and she shouldn't have tried. On the other hand, she could have been smarter about it. The "old" Kelly wasn't *all* bad. If she had loved and accepted the "old" Kelly more—his mellow attitude and raffish charm—and been less zealous in urging him to become such a perfect yuppie, Kelly just might have reached a different balance. If Gail had changed too, they might still be together.

Gail, of course, couldn't have foreseen the outcome of Kelly's transformation, but she admits now that her priorities got mixed up. She got carried away with playing Svengali, without thinking about the direction Kelly's changes were taking him. When Kelly became a corporate executive, Gail's bohemian poet image no longer fit his requirements, and he went looking for a new woman to go with his new self.

Marrying Smarter—What's Really Important

What's important when you're twenty usually isn't that significant in your life when you're forty. Your priorities change. Your pre-requisites for a man are different. I remember the men I was in love with when I was in my twenties—an actor, a singer, an explorer. Lots of fun, but not one was real marriage material. Looking back, I can see how awful my life would have been if I had married any one of them.

The following is a typical list of a woman's prerequisites for a mate at ages twenty and forty. The main difference seems to be that for a forty-year-old woman, character is more important than looks. For a twenty-year-old, appearances are most important.

TYPICAL TWENTY-YEAR-OLD PREREQUISITES FOR A MAN

1. Cute
2. A great body
3. Likes to party
4. Drives a good car
5. Has hip friends
6. Isn't a nerd
7. Dresses right
8. Cool pad
9. Terrific dancer
10. Exciting
11. Dangerous
12. Not someone parents would approve of

TYPICAL FORTY-YEAR-OLD PREREQUISITES FOR A MAN

1. Stable
2. Dependable

3. Compatible
4. Shared values and beliefs
5. Flexible
6. Affectionate
7. Sexually compatible
8. Easy to live with
9. Easygoing, good sense of humor
10. Honest
11. Giving and able to share
12. Safe and sane, acceptable to family and friends

In addition to making choices based on our uncultivated tastes, there's another big problem about the men we pick when we're young. We're attracted to them because of their exciting, full lives and seemingly formed personalities—because we don't yet have those things on our own. Then, when we develop our own full lives and stronger personalities, we often find we've made a bad choice.

Andrea remembers when she was twenty and just divorced with a little baby. "I was all alone, and the thing I thought about most was being married. I wanted the whole thing, the husband, the house, the perfect family unit. I never anticipated being alone with a baby at twenty. I was frightened and desperate, and I was crazy for this older man of thirty-nine.

"He seemed to represent security to me. I came this close to marrying him. Now I'm forty, and he's sixty. Whenever I see him I thank God it didn't work out, because I wouldn't be the woman I am if I were with him. He seems so old, so paunchy, and he has a bad attitude about everything. He's sloppy and opinionated. I can't stand to be around him. I'm embarrassed to think that I was ever romantic about him."

No wonder so many women in their twenties are attracted to jerks. Look what their needs and priorities are. If you find that you're frequently involved with men who turn out to be disappointments, think about your priorities. What are you really looking for? Have your priorities changed?

Do your criteria for a husband reflect immature prerequisites you've really outgrown? Do you know exactly what you need now?

Often we know more about the new boots we're going to buy for the season than about the new man we want in our life. We know the color, size, material, height and even when we'd wear them.

The One That Got Away

It's important not to have a knee-jerk bad reaction to a good man just because he's not what you always thought you wanted. Almost every older woman has a story about the man she could have married when she was younger. Ali remembers a chemical engineer in college. "Glen was bright and passionate. We went together all through college, but I was a theater major and always wanted someone in the arts, someone who would understand my career. He went to work at Corning Glass in Corning, New York. I couldn't see myself living in Corning.

"After leaving Glen behind, I felt committed to following through and finding a fellow artist, but after years of crazy relationships with flaky painters and neurotic writers, I have to admit, they're just not marriage material. At least not for me. Maybe I made a terrible mistake. Maybe I should have married my college sweetheart."

So now, almost fifteen years later, Ali's starting to look for a man like her first serious love in college. It's funny, but what we thought we couldn't stand when we were younger often turns out to be exactly what we want when we get older.

When I was young, I was a lot like Ali. I turned my nose up at men like her chemical engineer, men who weren't in the arts, men who weren't different or exciting enough. I told my parents their country club and their Cadillacs were going to be the cause of the next revolution. Then I wound up marrying a man who's guess what—an ex-engineer who drives a Cadillac and belongs to a country club.

Louise had a similar experience.

"When I was twenty-two, I was living with Jack, a Stanford graduate, in California. We were thinking about getting married. We had picked patterns for silver and dishes, and I was planning a big wedding with all my sisters.

"Then, at the last minute, I backed out. I decided I was just thinking about marrying him because we were living together, but that I really shouldn't. Jack was an Episcopalian and I was a Catholic. He wanted two kids, and I wanted five.

"He was about to enter the Navy as an officer. He begged and pleaded with me to forget the difference in religion and go ahead and marry him. But I held firm."

At thirty-four, Louise met Bernie. Neither of them had ever been married before. Bernie had been brought into her company as a consultant, and Louise, as the firm's bookkeeper, spent many hours with Bernie going over the books. Bernie had never before dated anyone at a client firm, but he asked Louise out. Soon they were dating steadily. Louise remembers her hesitation about Bernie.

"At first, I wondered, could I really be serious about a man who was Jewish, overweight, not into exercise—so different from the men I'd dated before? But then I realized my tastes in men had been pretty superficial up to then, and if I looked at my real needs, Bernie and I actually had a lot in common. What I really wanted was someone I could respect as a businessman, a companion who shared my interests in music and the theater, and a good family man. Bernie was perfect. We married a year and a half later, when I was thirty-five and he was forty-four.

"So after rejecting an Episcopalian who only wanted two kids, here I am married to a Jew and with only one child. I can't imagine being married to anyone else, though, and I'm perfectly happy with one child. And the religious thing has become less and less important to me over the years."

What seems so important at twenty-two sometimes turns out to be meaningless when you're thirty-two—or forty-two.

Getting the Fantasy You Cherish

Even if we're not looking for the "perfect man," even if we expect some flaws and are willing to compromise, we women harbor fantasies about our future husband. Some of these fantasies are childish whimsy, easily left behind; some must be carefully traded off before you give them up; and then, occasionally, there's a "must have" fantasy that you can't live without.

Always try to fulfill a fantasy you've cherished for a long time—
if it's within reason. Pick out the most important fantasy you've had
about your future mate, just one, put it on your "must have" list
and then go after it. Often you'll have to give up several other minor
fantasies in order to get the one that's most important to you.

Belinda, a tall, stunning blonde with big blue eyes and a slim
figure, could have been a fashion model or an actress, but the minute
she opened her mouth, you knew she was neither. Her speech was
precise and filled with the flowery words of someone trying to impress people with her intellect. A terrible palimony suit with a
former lover left her shattered and insecure about whether she'd
ever find a man.

"I can't seem to meet anyone with my values and education. I
intimidate men because of my intellect," she told me, turning her
patrician profile to show off a neatly turned French twist and adjusting the skirt of her designer suit.

"Most of the men I meet are intellectually inferior to me. I've
dated, but I haven't been seriously involved with any man since
Pema. When I met him, he had just come to this country from
Indonesia. He was a brilliant physicist, but he was very insecure
and unsophisticated. I did everything for him. I taught him how to
present himself, and how to choose fine clothing.

"I taught Pema about U.S. real estate, how to invest and acquire
property. Over the years we were together, I helped him become
a multimillionaire, and then he dumped me. He was supposed to
support me while I went to medical school, but while I was away,
everything fell apart."

Belinda's fantasy had always been to marry a doctor, ever since
a childhood disease had put her in their constant company. Doctors
were the men she admired, the ones she looked up to and the ones
she respected and wanted to be around. Men who made decisions,
strong men, men who counted, men others looked up to. Her father
was weak and ineffectual in her eyes, a pawn to her strong mother.
Not the kind of man she wanted.

She dated all kinds of men, but if they were doctors, her heart
began to sing, she put up with all kinds of abuse, and she followed
them everywhere.

For a while Belinda drowned her need for a doctor in her own ambitions. After all, society told her that she shouldn't want to be *Mrs.*—of Dr. and Mrs. so-and so—anymore; instead, *she* should be the doctor. She plowed through years of premed courses and then moved to Mexico when she couldn't get accepted at a U.S. medical school. When her relationship with Pema blew up, she ran out of money and had to come back.

Belinda never became a doctor. She became a medical film-maker instead, working with and dating some interesting men in the business—editors, screenwriters, an executive at her film pro-cessing lab—but she was never really satisfied with any man who wasn't a doctor. It was at this point that she came to me for coun-seling.

"Why fight the obvious?" I told her. "You're never going to be satisfied with anyone unless he fits that one big fantasy of yours. Let's look at the rest of your criteria."

It was a fantasy "perfect man" list—a doctor who looked like a tall Robert Redford, a Catholic like herself, a perfect specimen of manhood in every way. My immediate reaction was that if she ever found a doctor who looked like that, he would have such an ego that she wouldn't be able to stand him for five minutes. She gave me a sharp little look, but then we began to discuss seriously what she'd have to give up in order to have a man in her life.

I pointed out that she was already meeting lots of doctors through her film business, and she could join a video dating service if she wanted to meet more of them. But she had to understand that if she wanted a real-life husband instead of a fantasy, she'd have to quit spurning every doctor who wasn't a "tall Robert Redford" and a "perfect specimen." After all, she'd been dating men who weren't even doctors, "just to go out." Why not "just go out" with a slightly imperfect doctor?

Belinda, claiming she'd never be happy with the results, never-theless agreed to try new criteria for six months. Her new criteria were a doctor who was single, attracted to her, liked by other doctors, and fun to be with.

Within two months she was madly in love. So suddenly, after twenty years of failure. I asked her if she had any misgivings.

"Oh no, he's wonderful. Not tall, but so caring, and we like all the same things. He's extremely intelligent. All the other doctors look up to him. I wouldn't trade him for anyone in the world."

It's funny, how a real man with imperfections can beat a fantasy "perfect man"—if you just give him a chance.

CHAPTER FOURTEEN

Nontraditional Choices

Once you reach forty, there are three single women for every single man your age, not counting the ten percent of men who are gay or the fact that many forty-year-old men want to date twenty-five-year-old women. If you've achieved some degree of success and want to "marry up," your odds are far worse.

On the other hand, if you're willing to fling tradition to the winds, you can improve your odds by looking for younger men or men who make less than you do, or both.

Marrying a Man Who Makes Less

How many times have you heard, "It's just as easy to fall in love with a rich man as a poor one"? Of course it is. The question is, who is *he* going to fall in love with?

Or, "Stand where it's raining pennies and you'll get covered in pennies; stand where it's raining dollars and you'll get covered in dollars." You can easily spot where the dollars are raining. It's where all those young, gorgeous, "killer" women are hanging around.

Just as many men seem to crave a *Playboy* centerfold, many

146

women seem to crave a man who makes a lot of money. Even women who have lots of money or are capable of making all the money they'll ever need seem to think they need a rich man.

Don't feel guilty if you, too, are looking for a man with a six-figure income. Once, when we needed a man to protect us and hunt for food while we were bearing children, it was important to marry a good provider. Today, a man's ability to be a good provider could be less important than his ability to love.

In today's society, for a liberated woman who doesn't really *need* a provider, "marrying up" could mean marrying a man who's better educated in music and the classics, or more entertaining, or more mature, or more loving and affectionate than she.

Money Isn't Everything

I often counsel women who have chosen men because they were doctors, lawyers or highly successful executives. Usually these women are lonely because their husbands or boyfriends don't have any time for them.

"He's not sensitive. He doesn't care about my feelings." This is a typical complaint. Or from a doctor's wife, "He spends all his time on his patients and none on me. I married him because I thought I'd get lots of attention, lots of caring. But I never see him."

So it's important to think about what kind of lifestyle you want when you choose a man. When a man achieves financial success, it usually comes from total commitment to a career or business, at the expense of a well-rounded life and time with his family.

If you're the type of woman who doesn't need a lot of time and attention from the man in your life, then you might be happy with this kind of man. On the other hand, most older women want a man who's going to be a good companion, not one who's gone all the time making money.

As you get older, going out to fancy restaurants is less and less important. Once you've achieved some degree of financial security, what you need is a man who gets home at a reasonable hour and enjoys being with you, who has weekends off for doing things and going places together.

"We never saw each other. He was running his business; I was building mine." Paula, age thirty-seven, was describing her last marriage. "Oh, his secretary would call mine so we could occasionally get together for dinner, and of course, we'd eventually wind up in bed together most nights, but we were usually too tired for sex. We had this great house, but the help enjoyed it more than we did.

"In eight years, we managed to get away for vacation together, without one or the other of us having an emergency come up, just twice. God, it was great—the plushest suites at the best resorts. Those were good times. But they weren't enough.

"I've been single now for four years. The business is exciting, and I'm proud of what I've done, but I want more. My clock is ticking. If I'm going to have children, now's the time. I know Ted's the answer, but everyone seems against me on this."

Paula, founder of a successful fashion manufacturing and importing firm, had come to me to discuss her plans to marry Ted, the new man in her life.

"He's a brilliant sculptor. I think he could sell more of his stuff if he expanded his little hole-in-the-wall gallery, but he really doesn't care about money. That's what I can't get anyone to understand. My mother, my best friends, my lawyer—they all think Ted's just after me for my money, for a free ride.

"Hell, I'd be perfectly happy making *all* the money, and Ted could be a house-hubby. He already is, sort of. I mean, we've been living together for six months, and we've set up a little shop out back for him to work in.

"What I really love is the fact that he's always *there* for me. And not just physically. I get home all frazzled, and he's so mellow and loving and soothing. He listens to me, encourages me. He's become my support system. I don't know what I'd do without him. But the best thing is, he wants a family, too. He just loves kids and wishes he'd had some, but his first wife couldn't. He'd be a great Dad. What do you think? Is everyone right? Am I crazy to want to marry this man?"

I told Paula she sounded totally sane and perfectly capable of making sound decisions about living her life. I did suggest, though, that she and Ted have a candid talk about the initial hostility coming from family and friends and be sure they were in full, comfortable agreement on how they would handle it as a married couple.

A little over a year later, I heard from Paula. She sounded exuberant. "Tracy, your reassurance was all I needed. I'm having it all!" Then, with mock chagrin in her voice, "Well, I did have to give up one thing—bringing the baby to the office for breast feeding just didn't work. But otherwise, everything's wonderful. Ted says he's never been happier or felt more creative, and even my friends have accepted him. In fact, most of my women friends are envious."

Samantha, a thirty-four-year-old foreign language translator with an advanced degree from Wellesley, had a different problem in "marrying down." She was from a wealthy East Coast family, and her profession, although it didn't pay well, was considered a socially acceptable occupation for a well-bred young woman until she married someone from a proper family.

"I've tried, but it never works," she exclaimed when she first came to see me. "I've broken two engagements to men my family approved of. I guess I've had a bad attitude problem since college. I always thought the Yale and Harvard guys were insufferably proper. Even when they were wild, it was just superficial. They'd sail around the world on a boat they bought with Daddy's money, and then they'd go right to work on Wall Street when they got back.

"I lived with an older man who had a successful real estate office, but he was Jewish and my family was concerned the whole time, worrying that I'd marry him. But it didn't work out.

"Now I have a real problem. I've found someone, really for the first time, whom I'm totally crazy about. He's bright, although he never finished college, and he's gorgeous—half Italian, half Portuguese, six feet tall, sexy black beard, hard as a rock. He loves me, and he's asked me to marry him. But he's a fisherman. He owns a fishing boat.

"He's met my family just once. He's very sweet, and he tried, but it was a disaster. My parents were all ripple-mouthed, trying to make small talk. Then my brother came charging through the house, screaming for our cook, asking 'who parked the foul-smelling pickup truck in front of my Jag?' I guess he thought someone was delivering fish. Sal has a wonderful philosophy on life, but it sure was put to the test that day.

"Later, I got into this crazy fight with my father. He hasn't spoken to me since. Mother keeps asking, 'What are you going to do, dear, when you have to stop working to take care of the children?' I keep saying 'We'll be able to get by on what Sal makes from the fishing.' And she keeps saying 'But, dear, you're not being realistic.' The same conversation, over and over.

"Actually, Sal's average takehome from the fishing isn't quite as much as I make now, but I've saved, and I can do translating part time. We can make it work. But how do I make peace with my family?"

I told her that peace might not be possible, and if she didn't love Sal enough to go ahead without family approval, she should postpone the marriage.

Samantha married Sal. Samantha's mother and brother both attended the wedding, in the brother's Jaguar, since her father refused to "have anything to do with my daughter becoming a fishwife." I got a note from Samantha recently. Her father suddenly melted when his first grandson was born, but she and Sal have maintained financial independence, getting along on his income. "We're still driving the old pickup, but I couldn't be happier."

Paula and Samantha both became happily married because they were willing to accept men who didn't fit traditional notions of "eligible." In Paula's case, the trade-off was mostly in terms of what people thought of her. Samantha, on the other hand, traded off her whole lifestyle for Sal.

Neither Paula nor Samantha, however, would consider their choice to be "settling for less." If they did, it would be a sure sign of trouble ahead.

But It Can Be Important

We women are all programmed to expect a husband to support us, or at least to make more money than we do. This expectation is deeply rooted.

If you marry a man who makes less than you do, you must have an absolute conviction that it's the right thing to do and have another reason for loving and respecting him. Perhaps he has a great intellect. Perhaps he's devoted to a cause. Or, like Ted is for Paula, maybe he's a wonderful support system for you, providing you with encouragement when work is difficult, support in the face of adversity and love and affection when you need it most.

If you think he's so gorgeous he doesn't have to do anything but lay there, or if he's such a great lover you're happy if that's all he does, you should think again. If the element of respect is missing, your love for him may slowly change to resentment. Your mother will never stop asking, "Is your husband working yet?"

Meredith, a typical boarding school princess who had everything she ever wanted and learned to shop at her mother's knee with her father's credit cards, fell in love with Barry, who makes much less than she does.

"He doesn't have to make as much as I make," she told me when she came to see me. "His tastes are much simpler than mine, and we keep entirely separate accounts."

Barry was Meredith's second husband. She'd married the first when she was twenty-seven, after they'd lived together for five years, more out of momentum than anything else. Within two years, they had divorced.

"We had the monogramed towels, the good furniture, everything, but it didn't help.

"With Barry it was different. Marrying Barry was a decision I made and followed through on, as opposed to having it happen to me. I chose to be in this marriage. I made an effort to marry him. It was a goal. I had lived alone a long time. My first husband was a lot like me. Barry is different.

"He's idealistic, and I'm materialistic. He comes from a hippy background. Money doesn't matter to him. Once I asked him about his dream job and what it would pay. It was some sort of research job on Cousteau's ship, the *Calypso*, and he'd be happy with $25,000 a year. I was shocked. Twenty-five thousand a year. That's all he wants.

"I don't mind paying my way. I grew up in a household where

my mother didn't make any money and had to hang around waiting for hubby handouts all the time. I don't have to hide under the bed when the Saks bill comes in like my mother used to, because I pay it. If I had to depend on Barry, he'd say, 'Here's five dollars, go buy a dress.'

"He thinks spending ten dollars on a haircut is a lot. I'll spend forty dollars and think I got a deal. If I went to Baha, I'd spend $150 a night for a hotel. When we were going together, he was looking longingly at this youth hostel. I told him, 'I'm not staying anywhere that doesn't have a bathroom.'

"I'm not wildly extravagant, but he can be very cheap. We engineer around it so it doesn't become a problem. We compromise a lot. We have separate accounts. I keep my money in one; he keeps his in his own. We both put money into a joint account for the household expenses. If he didn't put in his share, he knows I'd be really annoyed. I'm trying to get him to agree to a price so that I can buy half the house from him, because I want to fix it up and he can't afford to.

"Sure, I'd like him to earn enough to buy me nice presents, but it won't happen. I'd be upset if I expected a lot from him in that way. I don't expect a lot, so I'm not disappointed."

She paused, not certain how to continue.

"Here's the problem. Last Sunday he just announced, 'I've decided I'd like to teach. Maybe I'll go back to school and get my masters degree in philosophy. What do you think?' I'm supposed to be thrilled, I guess. I didn't know what to say. That's why I'm here.

"If he were sick, I guess I wouldn't mind supporting him. But I want him to work. I mean, he's tried several jobs and hasn't been happy with any of them. But I never thought it would come to me putting him through school."

Meredith and Barry had a serious problem. She had never fully reconciled herself to Barry being a low earner and what it would mean for their life together. This was apparent in the difficult negotiations over vacation budgets and her awkward attempt to gain total ownership of their home.

Worse, she had never fully understood Barry's lack of concern for money, nor did she have any deep respect for his potential as a person. When they came to see me together, he was dismayed. His decision to be a teacher seemed to him to be a sound career choice. He just assumed Meredith would be pleased that he'd finally made this major life decision. He couldn't understand why, to her, it just seemed to be more evidence of his flakiness.

Over time, Meredith and Barry were able to come to terms with each other. Barry agreed to get a part-time job while going to school so that Meredith wouldn't be solely responsible for supporting them. And Meredith learned to appreciate the qualities in Barry that had drawn her to him originally—his loving nature, steadfast loyalty and refreshing sense of idealism. She accepted the fact that as far as material things were concerned, she would have to provide whatever luxuries she desired. But the trade-off was more than worth it.

Marrying a Younger Man

Once, the only "respectable" solution to the lack of available men in the forty-five and over age range was to find some seventy-year-old man who thought of you as a young chick. Today, there's another option: Find a twenty-nine-year-old who thinks you're a foxy lady. For many older women, younger men are the new status symbol.

Advantages of Younger Men

Older women are turning more often to younger men for fulfillment and love. Younger men are more pliable, more liberated, more likely to respect your knowledge, more apt to let you be the boss.

Younger men are sensitive and sexy, flexible, flattering and full of life. They build you up and listen to what you have to say. Besides, there are so many more of them than there are men over forty-five.

Just as a man will pick a woman who looks good on his arm and who fits his image, an older woman now can pick a younger man to fit her image, to mold into her life. A younger man can be supportive, attend your business functions and help you look good at work. The right younger man will understand your ambition, be happy to share homemaking and child care and be a willing and able lover.

If you're secure enough, you don't need a man to play the role of wise father figure to tell you what to do. You don't need to be taken care of. Younger men are less macho, less concerned with having to be the older, richer, dominant, more educated part of a couple. The ease with which some young men slip into relationships with older women astonishes women who are trying this for the first time.

One woman in her fifties told me, "Divorces have left lots of women my age looking for new men, but the men in our age range all want younger women. Pretty young girls are a success symbol for these middle-age codgers.

"When I did go out with men my age, they never courted me. They just talked about their failures—their sex problems and their ex-wives and who did what to whom. But no matter how big a failure an older man is, he always wants to tell you what to do. I'm much happier since I started dating younger men.

"These younger guys really appreciate me. They feel like the women their age are airheads. Actually, I was an airhead, too, when I was twenty. Younger men aren't just looking for sex. They want someone to talk to, and they don't expect applause each time they get it up."

What to Look for in a Younger Man

Look for a younger man who has already found some success in life, despite his young years. That way he won't be crushed if he finds he has to play second fiddle to you once in a while.

Look for a younger man whom you respect, for his intellect, his warmth, his ability to love, his business acumen. Make sure there's at least one thing he does better than you do. Just as in loving a man who makes less than you, he's got to be more than a pair of cute buns; without respect, it won't work.

Look for a young man who wants to settle down, not some disco Johnny who will want you to party with him all night and think you're a drag if you don't.

Look for a younger man who has always been attracted to older women. That way some other older woman has already gotten him used to people's looks and relatives' complaints.

Look for a younger man who's had lots of young women and who's found them lacking. That way you won't have to worry about him leaving the first time some cute young thing wiggles around him.

Look for a younger man who adores you, who worships the ground you walk on, who really believes you're the most wonderful woman in the world. Then when your friends say he's just after your money, his adoring looks will show them wrong.

Jeremy, a thirty-year-old lawyer, is typical of the new unmacho males who bring joy to older women. He's intelligent, slight of build, looks young for his age and is disarmingly open about his preference for older women. He's currently engaged to a thirty-seven-year-old.

"The oldest woman I've been with was fifty-four. When I was nineteen, I fell deeply in love with an older woman of twenty-nine," he says. "She had two kids, aged two and four, and my father flew up to the University of Oregon to talk to me about ruining my life with an older woman."

There are several reasons Jeremy prefers older women. "As a lawyer, I spend so much of my day taking care of people and their problems that I want to relax and be taken care of when I'm done with work.

"I really love the way older women feel free to nurture a man. With an older woman it's more easygoing. There are fewer games. An older woman knows what she wants, and often it's been me. How can I argue with that? To be honest, when I was younger, I was attracted to older women because it was much easier to get them in bed. Now it's because I just like them better."

Jeremy, like other younger men, thinks about what he may be missing. "The older woman is flabbier," he smiles. "No doubt about that. If you have a fascination for taut bodies, you give up something to be with an older woman. But when my friends ask me how I can stand to make love with a less-than-firm body, I tell them that their twenty-five-year-old women are going to get that way someday too."

Jeremy is very secure and successful. He feels good about himself. He doesn't need a starlet on his arm to boost his self-esteem. Less confident younger men don't make good mates for older women simply because they have more of a need to "look good."

What the Women Say

You may experience some initial reluctance to get involved when you first sense a mutual attraction with a younger man. You may be afraid of what your friends will think, or you may be worried that he'll see how big your thighs are or the stretch marks on your tummy. You may even be embarrassed because you feel there are mother-son incestuous implications. Sometimes feeling self-conscious about being with a younger man depends on the neighborhood.

Betty, age forty-four, has always loved younger men. When she was forty, she moved from New York City to a small town in Vermont.

"I never felt embarrassed in the city," she says. "I remember when I was thirty-one, I had an outrageous affair with an eighteen-year-old. My daughter was four. They got along great. We'd all go out together, and people would think I was taking my two kids out to eat.

"There were embarrassing moments, but I weathered them privately. One morning I came out from the bedroom and my daughter and my lover were both watching Saturday morning cartoons. I kissed them, and they both smelled like Fruit Loops. It was embarrassing, but nobody but me knew about it.

"But when I moved to a small town, everything changed. Everybody knew how many kids I had and who was who. I was having a mad, passionate affair with a twenty-one-year-old cutie. It was okay as long as we stayed in the house, but then one day I was out shopping with my girlfriend and we ran into him. He was wearing these little white shorts and a polo shirt, and he looked so young. He came bounding over to the car and gave me a big hello, a hug and a kiss. I was sure everyone in the shopping center was watching. People have been talking about me ever since."

Betty has been worried lately about keeping up her image in front of a new younger man, Ansel, a more community-acceptable thirty-two-year-old.

"One night we were necking on the couch and I got a hot flash. 'What's wrong?' he asked. 'You're so hot. Are you okay?'

"Not wanting to tell him I was having a menopausal flash, I said 'I'm just so hot for you, baby.' But then, a few days later, during another necking session, he suddenly pulled away. 'What's wrong?' I asked. 'Your heart's beating so fast,' he said, 'I got scared. I thought you were having a heart attack.'

"I just mumbled something about how he got me so excited." Betty admitted to me.

It takes a very secure older woman not to worry about growing too old to interest her younger man. Marrying a younger man definitely isn't for the weak of heart.

"When we're together, I feel proud and beautiful," Julia, a rather plain forty-seven-year-old, told me about her younger husband of forty. But, she adds, it wasn't always that way. When they first met, she resisted the relationship.

"When Martin and I first met, he was a baby of thirty-six, and I had negative feelings about getting involved with him. I worried that he would be attracted to my daughter. He made me feel older, more conscious of my wrinkles and cellulite. I'd dated much older men before, and they always made me feel young on a physical level, even though they made me feel older on a psychological level. Yet older men tend to put down a younger woman's intellect, while younger men build you up.

"Now that we've been married for three years, I feel differently. I feel better being with my younger husband because he relishes my wisdom, experience and maturity. I'm valued for the inner me, the ageless part. I learned to feel really good about myself because I can look at a younger woman and realize she doesn't have as much to offer as I do."

Some women who marry younger men, however, report ongoing anxiety about keeping their looks up.

Sylvia and Scott live in Chicago, where he is a cameraman for the local television station. They've been married nine years and have a little girl. When their daughter was born, Sylvia was forty-one and Scott was thirty-five—not a big age difference, but enough to matter.

"I get a facial every two weeks, thirty-five dollars a pop; I wouldn't do that if I weren't worried about looking young," Sylvia says. Not the most secure person in the world, Sylvia, an attractive but not beautiful woman, was always sensitive about the age difference between her and Scott.

"I lied to him when we met. I told him I was only four years older, not six. After a while, I began to believe I was only four years older. I lied on my driver's license. Then when we thought we couldn't conceive and were trying to adopt a child, I was suddenly confronted with adoption forms in which you perjure yourself if you lie.

"That night I gave him the works in bed. Everything. I went up, down and all over on him. Then, when he was thoroughly exhausted, I showed him my passport. By that time, we'd been through so much together physically and emotionally, it hardly mattered anymore.

"When I had my little girl so late, I realized what a blessing it was to have a young husband to get up in the middle of the night to feed the baby. But when I was pregnant, I missed having an older man to lean on as a father figure."

Babies pose a definite problem with marrying a younger man.

"All the cute little Yuppies are having two or three," says Sylvia. "I know Scott would love to have more children, but I barely survived having one at forty-one. I'm starting menopause and he's not even forty yet," she sighs.

"He's a Yuppie. He's ambitious. He has a lot of dreams and ideals that no longer interest me. He dreams of moving to New York and working for "60 Minutes." I'm ready to settle down. I'm ready to give up my youthful dreams and settle for a comfortable reality. He's not," and here Sylvia echoes what other older women say about their young husbands: They are young and that's an inescapable fact.

Sylvia and Scott have remained in Chicago, and they've managed to stay together. The age difference never mattered to Scott; he just loved Sylvia. Other couples haven't been as lucky.

"Sometimes I look at him and he looks so very, very young." Ginny, age forty-five, was describing her husband, Ray, age thirty-seven, in her first visit to me. "I'm beginning to show my age. I have wrinkles, and I look at him and I think, 'My God, look at him. He looks like a kid.' I could see him with some gorgeous young thing.

"After we were married, when my mother found out he was only thirty-five, she said, 'You're terrible.' But I told her it was just something women didn't do when she was young, and that it's acceptable now.

"I went out with older men before I met Ray. These men would say, 'Let's try to make love.' And very often they failed. It's the other way with Ray. He doesn't fail, but I find that his energy level is hard to keep up with sometimes.

"And I always have to struggle to keep up when we're out hiking. Otherwise Ray teases me. He'll say, 'People your age need to rest more.' "

Ray's teasing was the tip of an iceberg of discontent. Soon, blaming a long commute, he was just coming home on the weekends. After that, he stopped coming home altogether. Ginny was devastated. She felt she was at fault for trying to attract a younger man in the first place and that her mother was right—she was terrible.

I counseled Ginny to stop blaming herself. Some relationships and marriages just can't be saved, and the problem may have nothing to do with an age difference between the partners. Often, when an older woman–younger man relationship fails to work out, the problem is that the younger man is opportunistic or immature or just plain nasty.

What to Avoid in a Younger Man

Evelyn, a forty-year-old therapist, went out with John, a twenty-eight-year-old, for two years. He moved in with her, and they became a couple. "At first, it was really flattering," she said. "I felt like John kept me young. For the first time in years, I felt sexually fulfilled. He said he was sick of young girls who always wanted something from him. He was relieved that I didn't expect him to support me. He respected me. He thought I was worldly, glamorous and sophisticated. He didn't think he knew it all.

"He said he wanted me to teach him things, and I did. Then after a while it became, 'Oh, you think you know it all.' We were on different levels of life. He appeared to be mature on the outside, but inside he really hadn't lived. Instead of older and wiser, I began to feel old and tired. About then, John must have figured he'd gotten his graduate degree in sex and life, and he just walked out one day. I was ready for him to go."

Then there are some men whom women should stay away from regardless of age.

Jessica, a New York publishing executive, talks about an admittedly bad choice. "Mario was adorable, but very immature. I saw him as a young Adonis, but he was selfish and mean-spirited.

"He'd go out with some younger people and then come home and tell me he found someone better and younger. He'd say he couldn't stay with me because I was too old to have kids. I was so hurt. Eventually I got the nerve to kick him out, but he cost me lots of money and all my self-esteem."

How Much Age Difference Is Too Much?

When Teresa, a fifty-two-year-old writer, fell in love with Jeff, a twenty-seven-year-old real estate manager, their friends were appalled.

"I just figured, let them be jealous. Jeff's so gorgeous, so tall, so thin, so healthy. They're just being mean because they don't have anyone. Lots of people just can't stand the idea that we're so happy," Teresa says.

When they began to consider marriage, she got worried. "I wondered if he'd want children at some future time," she said. "I worried about what my own grown children would think. One of them is older than Jeff." Teresa said she wouldn't marry Jeff until she got her weight down below his. She did, and they got married.

Teresa and Jeff have been married for two years now. Her children have gotten used to the idea. One of her daughters even volunteered to be artificially inseminated and have a baby for them should Jeff decide he can't live without kids.

"I wonder though," she says, "What's it going to be like when I'm eighty-two and he's fifty-seven? Is he going to be grossed out every time he looks at me? Am I going to be afraid to get undressed?"

Teresa's concerns will probably be put to the test before that, when Jeff reaches his midlife crisis years.

The Midlife Crisis Crunch

In most of the successful older women–younger men relationships, the man is still young. In fact, being happy with an older woman may be a young man's game.

All men experience some degree of midlife crisis as a normal life passage. At that point, feeling his youth slipping away from him, a man is most susceptible to the attractiveness of younger women. If he's already married to a younger, attractive woman, he's less likely to stray. If he's married to an older woman, he may find it more difficult to be faithful.

Charlie, age forty-three, a San Francisco investment banker, is married to Iris, a literary agent. "When she turned fifty," he said, "that really shook me up. To be married to a woman who's fifty years old! It really bothered me.

"I was a bit bothered, too, when I found out she'd been coloring her hair. I don't want her to be gray, of course, it's just that her age and her gray hair keep reminding me I'm not a kid anymore.

"Hey, listen, *I* still don't have a single gray hair, though, and I feel good about that."

The real crunch for Iris and Charlie will come not with her gray hair, but with his.

CHAPTER FIFTEEN

Getting a Commitment

What You Really Need

Gina, a bright, petite blonde stockbroker with twinkling green eyes, an off-the-wall sense of humor and a chirpy voice, was deeply in love with Stan, a moody but talented playwright. I had last seen her about a year earlier, when she'd started living with Stan.

"He still doesn't say he loves me very often, but I think he does. He's a terrific writer, but he's not that communicative in person.

"I've been doing a lot of work around the house. I've redecorated the bedroom, and I'm starting to tile the bathroom. I pay half the house payment and half the utilities. My investment is getting bigger and bigger, and we don't have any real commitment yet. Whenever the subject of marriage comes up, it's always vague, in the future. Then he changes the subject or says he doesn't want to talk about it now. Actually, he seems perfectly content to let everything go on just the way it is. I don't know how I'm ever going to get him to marry me."

"What is he supposed to do?" I asked her.

"He's supposed to propose! I want a proposal. I want him to

get down on his knees and beg me to marry him. I want him to bring me a big diamond ring in a little jewelry box. I want it all."

"And what would the outcome be?"

"We'd be engaged, and then we'd be married."

"So you want to be engaged. Then what you need isn't necessarily for him to get down on his knees and propose and give you a ring. What you need is an agreement. You need to get Stan to agree on a date to get married; then you can figure out the details. The rest is a Hollywood fantasy proposal you could probably live without. You could wait a long time for Stan to get the same fantasy in his head that you have. He may never get it.

"Have you told Stan that you really want to get married?"

"No, I'm waiting for him to ask."

Since I've known women who've waited many years for a man to propose, I told Gina it was up to her to raise the issue. She deserved to know whether or not Stan really was serious about getting married.

"You're going to have to tell him, straight out, that you want to get married. Pick the right time to bring it up. Be insistent. Let him know he's going to have to make up his mind and give you a date."

Gina and Stan were planning a weekend in Palm Springs. They'd been looking forward to it. We decided that an ideal time for a showdown would be in the car, halfway to Palm Springs, in the middle of the California desert. She would be calm and reasonable; he, a captive audience. He'd have to respond to her one way or the other.

Within five minutes, she had a date set. When he agreed, Gina gave him a big kiss. She didn't mention the wedding or the date again for the rest of the weekend. But she was triumphant. She was engaged.

Getting His Trust and Passing His Tests

Getting a man to make a commitment is like reaching any kind of agreement for a long-term contract. Both partners have to trust each other. Gina had already built trust with Stan.

Building trust is a step that automatically takes place in a relationship. As time goes by, you test each other. You check to see that he fulfills his promises. He checks to see if you really do what you say you'll do.

You're telling him about a book you've read. He says, "It sounds fascinating. I'll have to read it."

You say, "Don't buy it. I'll loan you my copy, but I need it back."

His test is to see if you remember to give him the book. Your test is to see if he actually reads it and then brings it back. If your relationship hasn't experienced lots of little tests about trust, money and reliability, it's more difficult to get a commitment.

You can set up tests. Make promises and fulfill them. Don't just say, "One day, I'll make you one of my famous Dutch apple pies," and then never do it. If you say you're going to do something, do it. He may never say, "Hey, where's the apple pie you promised me?" but he'll be thinking, "Are there going to be problems with this lady? She never came through with the pie, and she probably won't come through with other things."

How Long Should It Take?

You have a stronger negotiating position if you can wait him out—if time can be on your side.

Having time on your side means not rushing him. Let him rush you. Don't expect a whirlwind courtship leading directly to the altar in six weeks. Relax and let the relationship develop, get to know each other, build trust, and be sure that this is the right man for you. If you enjoy your time together without thinking every minute, "Is he going to ask me now?" he's likely to bring up the subject of marriage without any prompting.

On the other hand, you don't have forever. How long is it reasonable to play the waiting game? If you are over thirty, I suggest you firmly follow the two-year limit.

The Two-Year Limit

Assuming you are dating each other exclusively or are living together, if a man hasn't proposed marriage within two years, then you've got to force his hand, like Gina did. But getting an agreement isn't always as easy as it was for Gina. You may have to give him an ultimatum, and if he balks, you must be prepared to leave him.

I know this sounds cold and cruel, but I've seen too many cases of women waiting eight, ten, even more years for a man to decide he wants to get married.

The most exciting and obsessive part of the "in love" feeling usually occurs during the first two years a couple is together. This is when a man is most romantic—and most motivated to propose marriage. It also is enough time for a man to decide if he wants to spend the rest of his life with you.

Getting the Whole Story

But first, as you are getting to know him, find out his needs and requirements. You have to fill an important need for him so he'll become bonded to you.

Get his whole story. Let him tell you all about his life, especially his ex-wife or former girlfriends. This is a good way to find out what turns him on and off. Information about his old relationships will tell you what needs of his you can fill. What did he get that he didn't want? What didn't he get that he did want?

Does he want kids? How many? Does he yearn for companionship, for good conversation? Does he want someone to play tennis with, go to dinner with or hike and camp with?

For example, a man who is an only child or the child of a broken home, who didn't have a large and close family as a child, can be a good candidate for family seduction. Make him a part of your big family and offer him that which he's missed so far in his life.

Finding Out His Objections

If he loves you and is happy with you but he's not proposing marriage, there's something holding him back. You can't deal with the problem unless you know what it is. He may not want to tell you why he doesn't want to marry you, and often men don't, so you'll have to pry it out of him. Sometimes, only a demand that he commit will bring out his objections.

Finding out what's holding a man back from marriage doesn't have to be frightening or upsetting. In fact, you may discover that he actually wants to marry you—except he feels he should buy you a big engagement ring and he can't afford it right now, or he thinks he should wait until after his brother marries, or he's waiting for the lease on his apartment to run out. Or his objections could be more serious, like he can't stand your children. Or he wants kids and you don't, or vice versa.

When a man is hanging back, it's usually not because he absolutely won't marry you under any conditions, period. Usually, what's going on is that he doesn't want to get married under the present circumstances at the present time. Or he could just be waiting for you to tell him that he doesn't have to worry about whatever's concerning him.

You may have to drag his concerns out of him, but all the while he may be secretly hoping that you can overcome the problem and reassure him that you love him and that everything will work out fine. So instead of thinking, "Oh, that's it. He says he's not ready, and that means he'll never want to marry me," keep talking. Get his concerns out on the table and go to work on them.

Overcoming His Objections

Joyce, a thirty-four-year-old nurse, was living with Elwood, a divorced accountant. They had been living together for two years when Joyce began to press him for a decision on marriage.

First, Joyce reminded Elwood of how much fun they had together. Which he agreed with. Then she reminded him of how easily they had been able to work through all their problems so far, and she told him how much she loved him (all of which Elwood agreed with). Finally, she said, "So, I think we should get married next spring."

Elwood became very upset. "Everything is so good. Why do you want to mess it up?"

Joyce countered, "Being married would just make everything better."

When they came to see me, we worked on finding out what Elwood's real objections were. "How would marriage be difficult?"

"I can't afford to get married right now. I want us to wait until I can afford a wedding, a honeymoon, a house to live in," Elwood replied.

"I can't wait that long," said Joyce. "Besides," she added, responding quickly to his concern, "You should marry me now—that way you'll know I'm not after your money because you don't have any."

By knowing Elwood's secret concerns about marriage and money, she was able to reframe his objections and turn having no money into a positive instead of a negative.

Elwood knew Joyce had a point. After much reassurance from Joyce that having money wasn't important, that she would be happy to plan a simple wedding and that she could borrow a friend's condo in Vail for their honeymoon, he agreed to set a wedding date. He was actually relieved because he very much wanted to marry Joyce, but he was waiting to be convinced.

When He's Afraid of Losing His Freedom

Men are often hung up about marriage because they're afraid of losing their so-called freedom. When a man says he's afraid of losing his freedom, it's important to find out exactly which freedoms he fears losing. Then you can reassure him he won't be denied his poker game, football or night out with the boys.

If it turns out, however, that the freedom he wants is to keep open his options for picking another woman, or if he's dead set against kids and having children is one of your life goals, then you may have an insoluble problem. If you do, be glad you found out, leave him and get on with your life.

As the song says, "Breaking up is hard to do." But leave you must, to give yourself a new chance at happiness—and, just possibly, to wake him up and cause him to change his mind.

The Power of Leaving

If a man doesn't embrace marriage voluntarily and can't be negotiated into it but is nevertheless potentially willing to commit, your leaving can act as the shock treatment he needs to see the light. Go away for a while; let him see what life is like without you.

One thing that a man really hates is to lose someone he believes belongs to him. He'll be imagining you doing all sorts of things you probably aren't doing. He'll be missing you. If he's ever going to want you, he'll want you back, on your terms.

In my private practice, I have almost as many men as women, but the men's problem is almost always related to getting a woman back.

Kenny, a cute, thirty-two-year-old, never married, Irish Catholic, was totally bewildered when he came to see me.

"I was with Megan for four years. She was always begging me to marry her. It made me feel good, somehow, with her asking me. I felt like I had the power in the relationship. She'd be saying, 'We should talk about our future, about getting married and starting a family,' and I'd say, 'Don't rush things,' or, 'Why can't you let it be my idea?' or 'Give me time.'

"Then I got transferred to Seattle, and she stayed behind, in graduate school in Ohio. We communicated by computer. She was nagging me all the time on the computer about getting married, and I'd put her off. Then, one day, I'd decided I would ask her, and we were talking on the computer and I sent her a message that she misunderstood, and she wrote back something angry and then I got mad, too. So naturally, I didn't ask her.

"It wasn't more than a month later, when I was about to ask her again, that she told me she had met a college professor she liked a lot. He was an older guy, and she was going to see if it worked into a real lasting relationship.

"I was shattered. I sent her a ring. She returned it. She said we could get another one if things didn't work out with her professor. I told her I was sorry. I begged her to reconsider. I think I may have made the biggest mistake of my life by not marrying her. I'll do anything to get her back," he pleaded. "Anything!"

His wasn't an unusual story. Time and time again men have told me how they didn't appreciate how much they loved a woman until she left them.

If you're with a man who has a fear of commitment, or who resists your sweet persuasion and stubbornly sits on the fence, or who has told you flat out he isn't going to get married, leaving is the best course of action.

Tell him firmly that you're leaving him because he won't commit. Let him know that as far as you're concerned, the relationship is over. Tell him you're going to find someone who can commit.

Make sure that he doesn't think you're leaving him to "make" him commit. *Don't* make it sound like a threat. And quit negotiating. The reason to give up arguing is simple: If deciding to get married is this difficult for him, he's got to feel it's *his* decision, not one that you forced on him.

So just leave. This is the best course of action for several reasons:

1. You really do have to get out of this relationship to make sure it doesn't drag on for years and years and ruin your life.

2. By telling yourself it's over, you give yourself the freedom to start looking for another man.

3. You leave the monkey on his back—you're no longer begging or threatening him—and he's alone with his thoughts.

4. If he then changes his mind, you're in a very strong position instead of a weak one. Then you get to lay down conditions instead of simply accepting them.

5. If he doesn't change his mind, you are already on the road to recovery.

Shock Treatment

Breaking up and leaving are the relationship equivalent of electroshock therapy. Knowing that it's necessary doesn't make it any less traumatic. But that's how Bonnie, age thirty-six, finally married

Brady, age fifty, a successful real estate developer, after a long and rocky relationship.

When Bonnie came to see me, she admitted that when she first met Brady she wasn't really looking to get married and she felt okay with just dating. "But I knew Brady was the kind of man I could marry," she said, recalling the beginning of their relationship. "He was everything I wanted.

"We went out twice, and he said, 'Call me. I'm in town on Mondays, Wednesdays and Fridays.' That turned me off. I thought, 'No way will I call you.'

"So I waited him out, and finally, he called. I was delighted when I heard his voice. Then he told me he was dating someone else. When she found out that we had seen each other a couple of times, they had a big argument about it and he agreed not to see anyone else for a while.

"I said, 'Oh, no problem.' I thought he was a little out of line anyway, thinking that after two dates my heart would be broken or something.

"Then three months later, he called and said that the other relationship hadn't worked out. You can see why I didn't want to rush into anything with this handsome, love 'em 'n' leave 'em type. We dated for about six months, and then I moved into his house in Malibu.

"We had an absolutely idyllic life, except for one thing, the 'M' word. Brady couldn't say it to save his life. At first, that didn't bother me at all. I had had lots of boyfriends. I didn't think of myself as being in a big hurry to marry.

"We were together for a year, the last two months of which we spent in Italy. One night, we were sitting in this romantic restaurant in Venice. Some Americans at the next table asked if we were honeymooners, and I said, 'Maybe next trip.' He immediately started acting weird, and finally I asked him, 'Is something bothering you?'

"He said, 'Let's wait until we get back to talk about it.' But I realized it would be three weeks before we'd get back, and I didn't want to spend the whole time wondering what was wrong, waiting for the ax to fall.

"So I pressed him. He said, 'I'm not that interested in getting married. I've been married twice and I'm scared of it, so let's just leave things the way they are.'

"I felt like he'd hit me in the pit of my stomach. I had known he wasn't eager to get married again, but I thought I was winning him over. And I'd let myself be so vulnerable with him. I cried, on and off, for days. I couldn't stand being away with him knowing how he felt. We cut our trip short and flew back.

" 'Does this mean it's over?' he wanted to know. I don't know why, but that made me furious. I told him I didn't feel that life held any great guarantees, but I didn't want to have a guarantee of nothing, no future.

"When we came back, I went to see my family in Washington. I was so torn. I still loved Brady, but I hated the lack of commitment. Even so, I moved back into his house in Malibu. We were living two separate lives under one roof. He was no more committed than he'd ever been.

"Most of the time I was okay, but once in a while I'd get depressed and I'd think, 'What am I doing here?' "

It was at this point that Bonnie came to see me. She was also worried about her career.

"Living way out in Malibu, it takes so long to get to town. My P.R. career's going down the toilet. I'm freelancing, but even so, you have to be in town on a daily basis."

Bonnie was about to start a demanding job for a new client she'd been fortunate to get, and she would have to be in her office early and leave late. She needed to have her own place in town. I advised her that this was the time to make a clean break with Brady.

Brady had a different idea. He wanted her to get an apartment in town, stay there during the week and come to Malibu on the weekends to be with him. He would have no commitment, no responsibility. But Bonnie had suffered a lot in this relationship, and she knew she had to get on with her life. She moved out.

"When he asked me, 'Are you coming out this weekend?' I was ready for him. I told him, 'No, I'm not coming this weekend, or any weekend.' I said that I finally realized I was not getting what I needed. 'I don't want to be your weekend girlfriend.

" 'So why don't you fly off to Acapulco and the Riviera or wherever and experience all the blondes and the redheads you want,' I told him. 'You need to go and live out whatever it is you think you'd be missing with me. But you might as well know that even if you meet some really fabulous gal, eventually she'll want what I want —normal things like commitment, marriage and children. I need a commitment. So I'm leaving. You do what you want to do.'

Bonnie didn't see Brady for about two months. "This is the hardest thing I've ever done. I miss him desperately," she told me. "I threw myself into my work. I convinced myself he was out of my life forever. Then he called and said, 'Can't I see you? Can't we just have a light evening?' And I said 'No.' And he said 'What if I moved into town and we got a place together?'

" 'I'm not looking for a convenient setup,' I told him. 'I want a marriage and a commitment, and I'm not interested in anything else.'

"He got angry. 'Are you telling me that you won't be available when I come around? What are you doing, punishing me, giving me my just due, showing me?'

" 'I'm just not available for dating,' I told him.

After that, Brady would try to see her with excuses like, "Meet me to pick up your mail." She succumbed to this twice. They had lunch, she got her mail, but that was it.

Then, Bonnie reported, "After another month or so, Brady called and said, 'I'm really missing you.' When I first left, he said he was 're-lieved,' and I had thought, 'Oh yeah, twist the knife.' So I said, 'I thought you were relieved.' That got to him. He kind of opened up at that point and told me he'd been having a lot of second thoughts.

"He'd been out with some other women and didn't have a good time," Bonnie went on. "He said he went to see a movie, *The Unbearable Lightness of Being*, about how this philanderer had to choose between satisfying his appetites or making a commitment to what is good and right, even though it's not always the easiest way. He said he'd decided that something was wrong with him and that he'd gone for some counseling to overcome his hangups about marriage. He sounded so sincere I agreed to have dinner with him the next night.

"He showed up dressed in a suit and a tie, with his hair all combed and a big magnum of champagne and a corsage for me. I hadn't had one since high school. He was carrying a big tape player. I saw all this equipment and didn't know what was happening. Then he popped the champagne and put on a tape of 'The Rose'—'It's the heart afraid of dying, that cannot seem to live'—or something like that. It was the story of his emotions, he said. Then he proposed to me.

"I guess it was a combination of therapy, the movie and my being very clear with him about what I wanted—and mostly my moving out. I was able to leave him because it was my only choice. I loved him, but I didn't want to be his doormat or sacrifice my life to his fears."

Brady felt he was getting a lot out of his therapy, and he asked Bonnie to go with him to a session or two. They stayed in therapy together until they went on their honeymoon. The therapy helped them both to get over all the pain they'd been through.

Bonnie and Brady got married in June, three months after Brady proposed. Brady rented out the house in Malibu and bought a house close to town in Toluca Lake for the two of them. "We're very happy. He seems totally content," she told me.

Coming Back

If you leave and then he agrees to get married and you come back, it's up to you to make sure he follows through. Don't let him think that he's got you back and that he can now return to his noncommittal ways.

CHAPTER SIXTEEN

The Wedding and Honeymoon —Older, Grayer, but Still Excited

When I was in my twenties, I thought that if I ever married, I would elope in a wild moment of passionate, uncontrollable abandon, like cartoon character Brenda Starr running off at last with the mysterious man wearing the black eyepatch. I too would marry a romantic stranger, someone who would just sweep me away. Naturally, I wouldn't tell my parents until after we'd said our "I do's" and were safely on the plane for Paris.

Instead, a year and a half after meeting Marshall, my husband-to-be, we cautiously moved in together. A year later we became engaged. Then, after studiously avoiding anything to do with weddings or getting married all my life, I suddenly realized I needed a crash course in how to have a wedding. I began to buy *Bride's Magazine*, the bible of about-to-be-married women.

Looking at all that stuff in *Bride's*—the tulle, the cakes, the yards of white satin, the endless lists of what you should and shouldn't do, the preferred samples of invitations and matches and napkins with your names on them, the horrendously expensive cake toppings "of crystal and sure to be a lifetime momento"—seeing it all set off some sort of inexplicable primal urge in me.

I'm telling you about it so you won't be surprised if it happens to you. Suddenly, and with no explanation, I wanted it all. The works. My Brenda Starr fantasy of elopement was long gone. Early plans for a simple, backyard ceremony with a few close relatives and friends were out the window, replaced with arrangements for a baronial feast with musicians and attendants. There I was, at age forty-two, filled with the same bridal fantasies as a younger woman —flowers, white dress, veil, train, garter and bouquet. After all, I'd never had it before.

Getting married felt to me like an induction ceremony into the society of grownup women that I'd missed. I'd waited long enough. I was ready. I was sure. I deserved it.

Marshall, with three prior weddings behind him, gave me a warning. "You have no idea what you're letting yourself in for," he said. "You know less about getting married than any woman I've ever known." It was true. All fantasies aside, if I had married in my twenties, my mother would have thrown a huge wedding and arranged everything. That's what I thought she would still do. But I was about fifteen or twenty years too late.

My parents are retired and live in Palm Springs. My mother has a crowded schedule of golf games and bridge parties and a second career as a real estate mogul. When I called to tell her I was getting married, she went right to bed with a headache!

Like any mother with a never-married daughter in her forties, mine had made up terrific answers for her friends when they asked about me, like, "Tracy's working on a novel in outer Mongolia." Both my parents had fully reconciled themselves to the fact that their daughter was not getting married, ever. Now I was upsetting everything.

"I'm too old to plan a wedding," my mother groaned. "I live too far away. You'll have to do it all yourself." My father wanted to know, "Why do you want to get married? What's the difference?" He was alluding to our living-together state, of which he had never approved.

My parents' reactions were just the beginning. People just don't react the same way to a gray-haired bride. Some friends were shocked. Some were sad, and a few, still single, felt I was abandoning them. Others never said how they felt, but just made snide remarks like, "Are you going to be allowed to talk on the phone when he's home?" Of course, some were really enthusiastic, like the unmarried girlfriends who pleaded with me to aim the bouquet right at them. I considered throwing eight bouquets until I priced them.

Being a Bride

Marshall was right. Becoming a bride wasn't as easy as I thought. Soon I was faced with hundreds of planning details. And my friends weren't much help—either they were too old to remember their own weddings or they were long since divorced and preferred to forget the whole thing.

Choosing bridesmaids was another problem, since I had developed so many friendships throughout the years. Who would I feel closest to? Who would be hurt if I didn't ask them? Who would be the most help? And who, at our age, would wear whatever silly dress I wanted them to wear just to please me, walk where I wanted and look sweet, without any caustic remarks on the side?

Gifts were another hassle. Did I have to tell the store's wedding registrar that we'd been living together and had enough in our garage to furnish a country home? Couldn't we just sign up for a plumber or a new front lawn?

Even going to a department store bridal show with a friend proved traumatic. There we were—two gray-haired ladies among hundreds of mothers and young daughters. When I went to take a handout, the man behind the counter said chastisingly, "Those are for brides."

"I *am* a bride," I smiled bravely, trying not to be too angry or embarrassed. But my friend was looking at me with daggers in her eyes. "We don't *belong* here," she hissed. "Let's go shopping. Let's have lunch. I need a drink."

I dragged her over to the gift registry. "This is only for brides," the girl at the registry smiled sweetly. I couldn't say it again. My friend was pulling me away. Getting married for the first time at age forty-two was not like doing it at eighteen, and nobody was going to convince me that it was.

Nevertheless, I persevered in my desire to have all the traditions—to be given away by my father, to have a religious, spiritual and meaningful ceremony, to wear a white dress.

With talk of a white dress, my mother's interest in the proceedings came alive. After scouring her local stores for just the right feathered quill pen for the guest book and assembling a huge invitation list, she arrived to take me wedding dress shopping.

Marshall and I decided to be married by a rabbi—even though Marshall isn't Jewish and I'm not very religious, mostly to please my parents. Also, he had never before been married by a rabbi, so he figured, why not?

We spent two weeks looking for a rabbi who wasn't too religious, but was still spiritual and would marry us the way we wanted to be married. Would it be the "Zen rabbi" in Malibu? He talked to us about oneness and sang songs to us in Hebrew under his glass tetrahedron-shaped roof. Or the "Hollywood rabbi," whose walls were covered with autographed pictures of all the movie stars he had married. We also spoke to the "hip rabbi," who called me "babe" on the phone, and to the "assembly-line rabbi," who could fit us in between four other weddings that day.

Each rabbi interview was a study in awkwardness. There we sat, Marshall and I, in the rabbi's office. The rabbi would ask, "Is this your first marriage?" And I'd say yes, and he'd look at Marshall. "So, is this your first, too?" Marshall would simply answer "No," hoping the rabbi would stop there. But he never did. Instead, he'd say, "Second?" and Marshall would answer "Nooo," as if to imply that he could play this game as long as the rabbi wanted to. But by the time the rabbi got to "Fourth?" everyone was thoroughly uncomfortable.

Eventually, we selected the "hippie rabbi," a cantor who played the guitar. He was soft-spoken and gentle, and he agreed not to make the ceremony overly religious or use any more Hebrew than was absolutely necessary. After all, Marshall's parents had never even seen a rabbi up close, and we didn't want them to be overwhelmed.

Planning the Ceremony

The days flew by, and still we hadn't found a wedding site that would fit both our budget and our dreams. I was getting worried. Why hadn't I started planning a year ahead, I wondered? Why didn't anyone tell me how much work it was? Was this why most brides were so young? You had to be strong to stand the stress.

Finally, we settled on a rustic country restaurant that had long been a favorite of ours and where our friends and families would be comfortable. We loved the restaurant's large outdoor patio next to a rushing stream, with a raised gazebo just perfect for a marriage ceremony. We decided on an afternoon wedding, to enjoy the beautiful outdoor location, and because we both had elderly relatives who were barely able to make the wedding at all and definitely couldn't handle a late evening.

While my brain was filling up with wedding music, bridesmaids' dresses and guest lists, I was getting farther and farther behind schedule with my book, *How To Make a Man Fall in Love with You*.

My editor would call, demanding to know, "When will I have the manuscript, Tracy?" And I'd say, "Do you think we should have chocolate cake with white icing or white cake with chocolate?"

White tulle danced through my brain. The book wasn't done, and I couldn't think of anything but the wedding. I was getting more and more hysterical as "bride fever" collided with my book deadline.

Surviving Bride Fever

It was at that point that we discovered what really happens to a forty-two-year-old first-time bride.

Five days before the wedding, I was drying off from a shower when suddenly, my back went out. Totally. The pain was excruciating. I couldn't stand up. Suddenly, the crooked hem on my dress, the cake filling, the flowers—nothing mattered except being able to walk down the aisle. And then, as I lay there on the bathroom floor, I remembered. Our plan was to walk down a long flight of stairs, around a garden path and up another flight of stairs into the gazebo. I fainted, and Marshall carried me off to bed.

Marshall's daughters, Pam and Julie, arrived in the nick of time. They and my other bridesmaids found themselves with most unusual prewedding duties—massaging my back, running for pain pills and canceling any and all plans that required me to be on my feet. The rehearsal was off, the rehearsal dinner was off—hopefully, not the wedding.

My new stepdaughters fixed the dress hem. They even painted my toenails because I couldn't reach them. Our new family unit pulled itself together to overcome a crisis. Miraculously, I was on my feet again for our wedding. It was a beautiful spring day, and there I was, dazed with pain pills, but walking—down the long stairs, around the garden and up the stairs to the gazebo.

My wedding dreams were all coming true. I was in bride heaven, except that when I opened my mouth to say my vows, nothing came out. I couldn't believe it. I had promoted books around the world, been on "20-20" and "World News Tonight," and here I was—speechless.

"I could see your father's mouth go grim out of the corner of my eye," Marshall told me afterwards. For an uncomfortably long time, I stood there with my mouth open. Then there was a little squeak; then I began to giggle; then I started to cry. Finally, through my tears, I managed to repeat the rabbi's words, and Marshall and I were married. Afterwards, I was grateful to our videotaper, who kindly edited out the most embarrassing moments.

I was also glad we had decided to videotape our wedding. Between my hysteria and my pain pills, I could hardly remember a thing. Marshall claimed the words stuck in my throat because I was such a dyed-in-the-wool bachelor-girl type. He may have been right. As the limousine whisked us away on our honeymoon, I found myself strangely disoriented. For just a moment, I wanted the security of home. Being suddenly married after forty-two years of being single was indeed a shock.

The Honeymoon

Deciding on a honeymoon spot was a problem. We wanted a place neither of us had been with someone else, someplace that

would be "ours" without other competing memories. The Virgin
Islands were out; he went there with wife number two. Tahiti was
out; I'd been there before. Ditto for most of Europe, the Bahamas,
Mexico, California, Nevada and Colorado.

Eventually, we chose a traditional honeymoon haven: Hawaii.
I'd only been there with my mother before, and Marshall had somehow missed it entirely.

We all have incredible fantasies of what our honeymoon will be
like, and no real honeymoon can ever live up to your fantasy.
Honeymoon horror stories are everywhere. The bride gets sick. The
hotel room is awful, or the reservations are messed up. The hubby
has a waterskiing accident the first day and spends the rest of the
trip in a cast. And everyone has at least one fight on the honeymoon.
Actually, unless you keep your sense of humor, you can wind up
in honeymoon hell.

I know, I was there once.

We were on romantic Maui, and my bad back was just getting
well when we left for Hana. The road, which was a twisting, pot-
holed, all-day affair in 1983, has since been repaved. Back then,
though, the first thing anyone did when they reached Hana was go
to Hasagawa's General Store to buy a T-shirt that said, "I survived
the Hana Highway."

By the time we got to Hana, my back was killing me and my
teeth hurt from grinding them all the way as Marshall, a former
race car driver, "found the curves" or "drove in the groove" or
something like that. Passing us in the opposite direction, I could
see the grim faces of other wives returning from Hana, husbands
white-knuckled at the wheel.

After Hasegawa's, on the way to the hotel, Marshall just had
to "check out" the surf at Hamoa Bay, even though it was pouring
rain. I looked at the deserted, ominous little beach with huge
waves crashing against big black rocks and said, "Take me to the
hotel."

He did, and then he immediately headed back out into the
downpour to the beach. I went right to bed at the then-funky (but
since glamorized) Hana Hotel. The room seemed bleak with the
rain beating against the windows.

"I'll be back in an hour," he said, running out the door. Three hours later, he hadn't appeared.

I was scared, and I was angry. After I'd finally found someone to love, he'd gone off and killed himself on our honeymoon.

I lay there morosely in bed, my back aching, listening to the rain on the roof, wondering if they'd bring his body to the door or if they would just come and tell me about it. I wondered if there'd be a lot of blood. And who I would call—my old hippie friends from the Sixties living in the hills or my mother?

Then, about four hours after he left, he poked his head in the door. "Hi, Sweetie. Here I am," he chirped brightly.

I just glared at him.

"The car's still out there, though, stuck in the sand," he added matter-of-factly, as if his being soaking wet and three hours late without a phone call was nothing.

"How could you do that to me?" I cried. I was furious at him for scaring me so badly, but relieved that I hadn't called anyone. It was our first big married fight. He explained that there was no phone at the beach and he had to walk all the way back, but I stayed mad for days, imagining a lifetime of not knowing if my husband were dead or not.

I was also upset because he wanted to surf. My honeymoon fantasy was for him to be constantly at my side, cooing romantically in my ear.

Unrealistic Expectations about Honeymoons

1. We'll spend the whole time making love.
2. He'll spend the whole time looking at me lovingly.
3. We'll love being together every minute.
4. He'll be happy to be with me, even going shopping.
5. We'll be in ecstasy the whole honeymoon.

The Truth about Honeymoons

1. Even twenty-two-year-old newlyweds don't spend the whole honeymoon making love. For middle-aged honeymooners,

the expectation that you'll spend the whole time making love is going to go unfulfilled. Wedding nights are usually the biggest disappointment. If you're too exhausted to make great love on your wedding night, it's okay. You have the rest of your lives. If he doesn't carry you over the threshold, it's okay too. After all, wouldn't you rather save his back for more important chores?

2. Of course, we've all seen the pictures of honeymooners in magazines. We know what they look like. We've seen the in-love expressions on their faces. The way they look at each other, staring happily into each other's eyes, with eyes only for each other. Why shouldn't you expect your new husband to do the same? He will. But not all the time. Posing for pictures is one thing. In real life, your older husband will have other interests. He won't be able to take his eyes off the fancy sailboats in the harbor, or the waves he wants to ride, or the girls in tiny bikinis. Is that a reason to get upset? Of course not. You have him for the rest of his life. What's a few minutes of looking in another direction?

3. Spending all that time together can be a real strain. You're not used to it. Even if you've lived together a long time, you've both been busy with other activities. Work, cooking, cleaning, hobbies, pets and friends have been in your life as well as each other. Suddenly, you're alone together with no other plans except to be together.

4. The older your husband is, the less likely he is to want to do everything you want to do. He has his own interests and well-developed likes and dislikes. He hates shopping. He loves museums. He hates sunbathing. He loves tennis. Don't expect his loves and hates to change just because this is your honeymoon.

5. Hardly any couples get through a whole honeymoon without one fight. Some couples spend the whole honeymoon fighting and wonder why they even married. Don't be upset. Fighting and making up are part of every honeymoon.

For me, the missing-and-presumed-dead-hubby episode was the only upset on our honeymoon. Marshall and I feasted and frolicked through four Hawaiian Islands, but it took us the first ten days just to get relaxed. Three weeks after returning from our honeymoon, I was still sending out announcements and wedding pictures.

I never knew getting married could be so much work. Yet, no matter what the problems were, I'm glad we had a traditional wedding with all the trimmings. Marshall and his older, grayer, but still-excited bride will always treasure the memories of the most wonderful day of our life.

CHAPTER SEVENTEEN

Marrying a Man Who's Been Married Before

When I married Marshall, both our track records in the relationship area were so dismal that nobody thought we'd last. I knew I wasn't just marrying my husband. I was taking on the task of being third stepmother to two worldly and wild young women and fourth daughter-in-law to his less than enthusiastic parents. Today, after seven happy years of marriage, I know I made the right decision.

Men who've been married before make better husbands. They've already been broken in.

My husband is quite happy to pitch in around the house, and he does most of the cooking. But he wasn't always that way.

Quite a few years ago, when Marshall arrived in California with his new young bride, the first thing he did was rent an apartment and put her to work fixing it up. Then he immediately went out, traded in their cute new yellow convertible (her graduation present from her parents) on a used Jaguar, threw his surfboard in the back and headed for the beach.

Back then, Marshall was the typical sexist dictator husband, and his first wife was the typical compliant homemaker. She pretty much did what he said. And he pretty much did whatever he wanted to

184

do, hardly thinking of what she wanted at all. He was cute, but not *that* cute. I'm sure I would never have married him, nor him me, when we were younger.

Today, he realizes what a terrible male chauvinist he was, but back then he had never even heard the term. He was just out of school and had only his conservative parents as a role model. His mother did the housework, and his father went out and earned a living. There was "woman's work" and "man's work."

The sad thing is that in this day and age I'm still hearing the same kind of stories from young women about their never-before-married husbands. Times have changed, but many young men haven't. Sometimes it takes a divorce or two to raise a man's consciousness.

Maybe He's Learned

If the man you want to marry has been married before, don't worry, be happy. Be happy that he's already learned to put the toilet seat down. Be happy that an ex-wife has already pointed out his weaknesses, saving you the disagreeable task. He's been through relationship failure and divorce, a sobering experience for anyone. This time around, if problems come up, he'll be more willing to work at solving them instead of storming off to the neighborhood bar.

By the time a man gets to his second or third marriage, he's probably graduated from only being attracted to T&A who don't talk back, look like good breeding stock and meet his law partners' expectations. When a man chooses a first wife, it's often as a trophy to show off, a mother for his children or a support system for his lifestyle rather than a real life partner. In later marriages, men begin to realize that they need more than a denmother or armpiece to spend their lives with.

Roles are more flexible in marriages with men who've been married before. A previously married man is more likely to be a help around the house. He doesn't have to play "Father Knows Best," and you don't have to play the "little woman." He may even be happy to be a house-hubby the second time around. He'll be more relaxed about your success outside the home. He'll know there's more to life than dinner on the table when he comes home.

It is true, however, that second marriages are not necessarily better than first marriages. If, for example, a man had an unfaithful wife who cheated on him all over town, he could have trouble learning to trust his next wife. Or he may have cheated on his previous wife, starting a pattern of infidelity that could carry over into the future.

Whether your man seems to be a saint or a sinner, you'll want to know all about his experiences, past behavior patterns and present attitudes. Finding out is far easier if he's been married before. Marriages always leave a trail.

Instead of just listening to his side of the story, ask his friends. Don't sound like a detective, just say you want to understand him better so you can make him happy. Friends can't resist telling stories, especially if you and he are already living together or engaged.

Encourage your new man to talk about his ex-wife or ex-wives. Ask what they did that really bothered him, why they didn't stay in love. This information is invaluable. You'll know exactly what not to do.

Talking to His Ex'es

Try to make friends with his ex-wife or ex-wives before you get married, even if you don't think you'll want to be bosom buddies for life. You'll be surprised how much you can learn about him from them. Get the whole story, so you can guard against a repetition of whatever went wrong. You'll be better prepared than you could possibly be with someone who has no marriage track record at all.

An ex-wife also can give you lots of interesting information about your new man's family. She's your ticket to a short course in how to get along with his mother, father, brothers, sisters and kids. She'll also tell you if some of them were impossible to handle, saving you from wondering what's wrong with you if you can't deal with them.

When I started asking around about Marshall, I got lots of stories, and I was glad I asked. Once my vague concerns were replaced with solid information, I felt much better. I found out that he was on good terms with each ex, which always speaks well for a man. Actually, I decided, since each of his marriages had lasted longer than any of my romantic relationships, his track record wasn't much worse than mine.

After all, on my way to finding the man of my dreams, I had kissed an awful lot of frogs. With ex-lovers scattered all over town, who was I to complain?

Engagement to a Previously Married Man

When we got engaged, I initially thought it wouldn't make much difference that Marshall had been married before. I was convinced that it would only mean that he was older and smarter now than he'd been then, so he was making a better decision. It also would mean that he'd learned to give and to share, to see a woman's point of view, and he'd be more able to empathize with my problems. I figured he'd be better at problem solving because he'd already dealt with so many problems, and he'd be able to give me help with my career, my family and friends, my home and my life in general.

I was right on all these counts, but I was wrong about his being married before not mattering much. It made a great deal of difference from the minute our relationship got serious. First of all, how do you tell your mother you're going to marry a man who's been married three times before? Very carefully.

If you are going to marry a previously married man and you've never been married before, you'll find that his previous experience with marriage colors almost everything you do, starting with your engagement.

To you, getting engaged is the biggest, most important thing you've ever done. To him, it's not exactly "ho hum," but it's not a first either. Starting with our engagement, I could tell Marshall wasn't as excited or as nervous about the whole thing as I was. And he knew what to expect.

Marshall knew far more about weddings, receptions, parents, in-laws and getting married than I. He knew exactly the right words to say to both sets of parents. He told my parents that "he loved me and would take care of me and would keep me out of trouble" (which turned out to be the magic words for my father). I, on the other hand, told his parents that I was marrying so late because I had had "a lot of wild oats to sow," precisely what his mother didn't want to hear.

You can guess that Marshall's parents weren't especially over-joyed or filled with great expectations for their son's new marriage. Since they had already taken three other wives into their hearts, number four would be a little harder. I had to win them over slowly. I was determined to have good family relations, and I was especially courteous to them. You will find that extreme courtesy and a smile goes a long way with in-laws. You will also find that you have to demand respect for your new marital relationship from family and friends who are accustomed to your husband's previous wife or wives or to your former romantic attachments.

Marshall encountered some natural skepticism when he an-nounced our engagement to his friends. But he assured them this was his last marriage—that he'd finally gotten the right woman.

He also wanted to make sure that his friends knew he didn't expect more engagement or wedding presents, and he told them so directly. I, on the other hand, never having been married before, wanted the works, including presents. And since some of his friends still wanted to offer us a gift to express their good wishes, we compromised by registering for inexpensive items.

The "excitement gap" between you and your previously married man also extends to the wedding itself. Since he's probably had a least one big wedding, he'll prefer to keep things simple this time. On the other hand, if you've never been married, you're entitled to your dream wedding if you want it.

Complications

If you're like me, you won't want to skip any part of the wedding you've waited for so long. And if your previously married mate is like mine, he'll go along with a big wedding to make you happy, but he won't be as thrilled about each little bit of the ceremony as you.

We had to demand respect for our relationship from people who were used to our hummingbird lives of flitting from flower to flower. What better way than a wedding with all the trimmings? But this created another complication of marrying later—the invitation list. Some of the invitation list issues we dealt with and which you may face are the following: Should you invite ex-wives to your wedding? And what about his children from former marriages?

You can solidify your position in your new family by inviting his children from a former marriage, particularly if they are close to their father. After all, you don't want to be viewed as "another wicked stepmother" or someone who's "taking daddy away."

If the children are very young, you may want to invite their mother, just to cement your new position in her eyes, to show how gracious you can be, to show you have no bad feelings and to have child care so the kids don't disrupt the wedding. If at all possible, include the children in the ceremony. Little ones can be ring bearers and flower girls. Older ones, ushers and bridesmaids. Sometimes a son or daughter actually "gives" away the parent during the marriage ceremony.

Marshall's two daughters, Pam, age twenty-two, and Julie, age twenty-three, who had not attended any of his previous weddings, were bridesmaids at our wedding.

Marrying someone who's been married before means you'll have to make those delicate decisions about which ex-wives to invite. We decided not to invite any ex-wives, but we did call and tell them that we were getting married even before the invitations went out, because we didn't want them to hear about it from others. We decided only to invite those ex-lovers who were friends with us as a couple.

Marshall's ex-wife number two happened to be in Hawaii when we arrived there for our honeymoon, so we had dinner with her there to celebrate our wedding.

I can already hear your gasps of horror. Celebrating with ex-wives? Inviting former lovers! What about jealousy? Competition? Fear of the other woman?

Handling Jealousy

As a new bride, you can afford to be generous of spirit at the happiest moment of your life. This means not being jealous of his past. It means welcoming his children. It means encouraging him to keep in contact with his former wives, particularly when children are involved.

Not only is jealousy mean-spirited, it is also useless. The other woman isn't hurt or made uncomfortable by your jealousy. You are, and so is your husband. Jealousy is a form of hostility that boomerangs, hurting the person who is jealous, not the object of the jealousy. Since the past is over and you have him right now, I suggest you make a pact not to be jealous of anything in his past that you can't change anyway.

When you marry a previously married man, just remember that it's a little different for him. He may not remember to carry you over the threshold, or he might have a bad back from carrying too many others! Or he may think the whole thing is silly. Remind him that it may seem silly to him now, but it didn't the first time, and this is your first.

Whatever you do, keep your sense of humor. Don't fight over the wedding. Compromise, negotiate. The important thing is that you get married, not that you have every bit of wedding hoopla that was ever invented. If he really feels uncomfortable with throwing the garter, skip it. Garter throwing is not essential to staying married. On the other hand, you should throw the bouquet, and the garter too, if you want. Have fun. Don't let worrying over unimportant details spoil your day.

Remnants of His Past

You will find that many of your previously married mate's patterns and habits are already set from his first marriage. This isn't necessarily a disadvantage, since former wives sometimes teach husbands good habits. He may bring you flowers all the time because that's what his former wife thought was romantic, and you may just love flowers. Or maybe you prefer an occasional dinner or show. He may think making love in the morning is terrific because that's the way "they" always did it. He may have a particular sex act she always loved that you could live without.

What's important is that if you disagree with any little habits or preconceived notions left over from his former marriage, you must speak up right away. Otherwise, by your silence, you will be agreeing with the way he always did things. And you'll be setting a bad precedent for the rest of your relationship.

Your previously married husband may have already experienced the "first time" nesting thrills you're looking forward to. He has probably already purchased and decorated his first home. He may have even lost a home in a messy divorce, so the act of nesting doesn't have the purely blissful connotations in his mind that it has in yours. Things that seem sentimental to you—buying your first pieces of furniture and getting your first pet—may remind him of things he fought over in the last divorce. So be sensitive. Find out how he feels about these "romantic" purchases.

Better yet, be creative and find new things the two of you can share that won't be associated with his old memories. For example, if he always spent New Year's Eve at crowded parties with his first wife, perhaps you can change the routine with a romantic evening at home for just the two of you. Or maybe you can go out of town on a romantic holiday.

Just be sure it's really a "first." You may be disappointed when you find that they did so many things together you had fantasized about doing for the first time with your new husband. Vacationing in Puerta Vallarta? Already done. Skiing downhill in fresh Colorado powder? Already done. Taking his first son for his first haircut? Already done. And on and on. Whatever you want to be first at has already been done. He may even have called "her" the same pet name he calls you. You may find other uncomfortable reminders of your husband's ex creeping into your life.

Anne, a forty-one-year-old teacher, married for seven years, told me, "It's the little things that bother me. I hate that mail still comes addressed to him and his ex. It bothers me a lot that she still uses his last name too. But there's nothing I can do about those things. I try to ignore them only because I don't want to fight over them."

It's easy to get angry and resentful, like Anne.

Don't. Just accept the fact that your secondhand husband will come with lots of baggage—kids, in-laws, families upon families—like a blue plate special where you get the potatoes whether you like them or not, no substitutions. It's all a part of him; the man you fell in love with is made up of all those past experiences and people. After all, without his past, without the women he loved before you and the life he lived, he wouldn't be the man you love today.

If ex-wives become so demanding that your husband is spending too much time or money on his former family, sit down with him and negotiate a budget for both. Agree on how much time and money are okay for him to spend on his former family.

Remnants of prior marriages will crop up in all sorts of ways—possibly as fears and insecurities left over from his past. If his ex overspent and ran up huge bills on his credit cards, don't be surprised if he worries that you may too. Gently, firmly explain to him, "I'm not her, and I don't overspend." Eventually, his concerns will be eased.

We all hate being compared, but remember, sometimes you might be—just as you compare your husband's behavior with that of other men you've known—your father, former lover, even a brother or a friend's husband. If you're sensitive to his "sore spots," though, the comparisons will be favorable for you.

For instance, my husband gets upset if I'm late; it reminds him of an ex. He worries if I'm too career-oriented; this reminds him of another ex. He worries if I'm overly concerned with looks or youth, because he thinks I'll be on the way to the plastic surgeon like one ex-wife. Even after seven years of marriage, these concerns are still in the back of his mind. So I just make sure to remind him that I also hate to be late, that I'm in no danger of becoming a workaholic and that I don't believe life is a beauty contest, so he can relax.

On occasion, he still thinks about treasures left behind or missing: the great condo he lost in a divorce, the deep powder skis that never turned up; the glued-together hairbrush broken once in an argument with an ex-wife which he intended to keep forever as a symbol of how upsetting arguments can become, or the ceramic mug made by an ex-mother-in-law whom he still admires. I sympathized over the condo, bought him a new brush, and we still have the mug.

The remnants of your husband's past diminish with time, becoming negligible intrusions on the new life you build together. But his children are forever.

Stepchildren

When you marry a man who's had children before, you become an instant stepmother to a child who probably either resents you or is indifferent to you. If you imagine you're going to be moving into the bosom of a ready-made, loving family, your imagination is running wild. Sure, there are lots of rewards to step-parenting, but they can be a long time coming. Don't expect the little darlings to fall madly in love with you right away.

The problem is that your stepchildren have no reason to be thrilled about their father marrying you. Basically, what they'd really like is for their Mom and Dad to get back together again, just like before. You're a stranger they're being forced to cope with who is stealing time and affection from their father and complicating their lives.

If you marry a man who's recently divorced from the children's mother, you're the woman who took Daddy away from Mommy. These children may have heard all kinds of terrible things about you from their mother, particularly if she's still alone and angry. They may be primed to hate you with all their hearts, while visions of loving motherhood are dancing in your head.

On the other hand, if your husband-to-be has had other wives since he divorced his children's mother, your more grown stepchildren will view you as just another of "my father's wives," amusing cocktail party gossip, or, if they're typical teens, "That's why we're so messed up." After all, how could they be normal when their father keeps marrying all these women?

Stepchildren in this situation have little vested interest in seeing you and your new husband make it as a couple. After all, they don't expect you to last any longer than the others. They don't want to get too close because they've tried in the past and been hurt. They think you, too, may soon be gone.

Your husband also may have equally rosy visions of resuming full-time fatherhood the day you return from your honeymoon. The wiser course is to rein in your parental urgings and let their mother keep them for a while. You and your new husband will have enough to do adjusting to each other without the added burden of raising children who are divorce-traumatized.

Yvonne tried so hard to make her new stepson, thirteen-year-old Victor, Jr., a part of her new family. He gave the toast at their wedding. He was the best man. He was loved and fussed over by all the bridesmaids. He was doted on by Yvonne.

She tried to ignore the fact that the boy's mother had tossed him out and had warned that he was violent. At first, he was really nice to his new stepmother. But it didn't take long before he pushed her down the steps of their condo and threatened to kill her. He caused so much trouble between Yvonne and her new husband that they had to separate until they were able to send the boy back to his mother in Chicago.

"It was a nightmare," she told me. "I thought I was going to help him grow, help nurture him, help him with his problems. I would be a substitute mother, making up for the crazy, abusive mother he had just left. I knew I would never have any children of my own, so I began to take all my mothering instincts out on Victor, Jr.

"It soon became obvious that he was just interested in what he could get from us. I couldn't believe that a child could be so mercenary. In the end, I was afraid of him. And Victor and I were having some problems too, partly because of Victor, Jr. I'm just so glad he's out of our lives. And I hope to God he doesn't come back."

Virginia, another of my clients, went to therapy with her new stepdaughters after their mother in Atlanta sent them back to live with her and her new husband. Even though she'd only been married to their father for a few months, Virginia welcomed the two girls into her heart. She gave endless love and affection and showered them with gifts. Virginia's parents, who had no other "grand-children," also gave them love and affection and showered them with still more gifts.

When they got involved with drugs, Virginia bailed them out. When they were unruly, she took them to family therapists. "I'll never forget what it was like at those terrible family therapy sessions," she told me. "I'd pour my heart out and the girls would just sit there and stare at me hatefully. They didn't want to try to work things out. They just didn't care if we were a family or not."

Advice on Handling Stepchildren

Insist on respect, especially in your home. You and your new husband must agree on rules for the children and expect them to be obeyed.

Regardless of what you suspect their mother may have said about you, try to make friends with her. If you and your new husband don't communicate with his ex-wife, you leave yourself open to all kinds of manipulation by the children. They'll get money for the same school books from you both, you'll be told, "My mother said I could," when she didn't and they'll tell her you said something you'd never dream of. Communication is the key.

Don't try to be a parent. Become a friend instead, and don't try too hard at that. Don't rush them with affection. Let them come to you. If you seem too anxious for them to like you, they may withhold their affection to see what you'll do to get their love.

Eventually they'll get curious about you. Then you can show them what a nice person you are.

When I first became a stepmother, Marshall's daughters pitched in and helped at the wedding and were very friendly, but it was more because they were good sports than because they were embracing me. And who could blame them? After all, they'd already gotten close to two other stepmothers, and what happened? Divorces each time. They were a little wary of getting close again.

While I was careful not to get between them and their father and mother, I listened to them and offered advice when they wanted it. Gradually, we became friends. The process took several years, but I knew they had finally accepted me when they began to tell me things they'd never dare tell either of their parents.

Now, although I'll never really be a mother to them, I feel as if we have a very special friendship. I was touched when Julie sent me a Mother's Day card to "My Other Mother," especially when I was feeling sorry for myself, thinking, "I'll never get a Mother's Day card." And I felt really cared for when I was on a book tour in Seattle and Pam met me at the airport with a beautiful long-stemmed rose and we went out for a fancy dinner at the Four Seasons' Georgian Room.

Recently, both Pam and Julie were married, and I was proud to be in the front pew with the close relatives. Over the years, we've grown to love each other. After all, we both love the same man, their father.

You won't be alone dealing with the problems of stepchildren. Your new husband will be your partner, bringing his experience as a parent, a healing love that bridges your differences and the knowledge that time can work wonders.

Not just with the children but in all aspects of your marriage, your previously married husband will contribute perspective and realistic expectations. He won't expect you to be perfect, and he'll know he isn't. He'll also know exactly how good things are with you, not compared to some fantasy in his mind, but compared to a real-world marriage experience. He'll try harder because he doesn't want to fail again. You can have the best of all possible worlds—the advantages of his past experiences, together with his present love and appreciation.

CHAPTER EIGHTEEN

Marrying When You've Been Married Before

In some ways, marrying again is easier. You're used to living with a man. You don't have to start learning how to share or to say "we" and "ours" instead of "me" and "mine." Your selection of a husband should be wiser. You don't expect your husband to be Superman. Loving, kind and considerate will do just fine. You're more willing to compromise and to work things out. You're not as eager to rush into marriage as those who've never walked down the aisle. You're more aware of marriage's rewards, sacrifices and problems.

On the other hand, you've suffered through either divorce or the death of a husband. There is no easy way to end a marriage.

Even when I hear, "It was just signing papers. The feelings had been gone for a long time," I know these words cover a volcano of buried emotions and a deep sadness over wasted years. But the past is the past, and the sooner after your divorce you think about remarrying, the better your chances are. Like falling off a horse. The sooner you get back on, the easier it is. You won't have time to build up unreasonable and irrational fears.

For some women, however, the fears are not so unreasonable.

When Your Last Marriage Was Lousy

It's certainly natural to be worried if you've been married before and it was awful.

"I'm so nervous. My life will be over if I get involved in another horrible marriage," thirty-three-year-old Audrey, a successful New York real estate agent, confided to me just one week before her wedding to Spencer, a forty-year-old, divorced psychologist. Audrey's first marriage had been so bad she thought she'd never get married again.

Even though her fiancé, Spencer, was nothing like her former husband, Audrey was worried. "In my first marriage, I was constantly terrified. I never knew when he'd lose his temper and blow up at me for no reason. It was a nightmare. He'd be screaming at me and slapping me around, and I'd be feeling guilty, thinking that the marriage was failing and that it was my fault and that there must be something I was doing wrong."

"Can you imagine Spencer losing his temper and hitting you for no reason?" I asked her gently. Her face softened somewhat. "Of course not," she said. "But Joe seemed nice, too, before I married him. Maybe marriage does something to men. I know that's silly, but I just can't forget those awful years with Joe."

When I talked to Audrey again after she and Spencer had been married a year, I asked her if she still worried about Spencer turning into the monster that Joe had been. "I can't imagine how I ever compared the two men," she laughed. "Spencer would never act like that."

People who've never been married have no idea how bad marriage can be when it doesn't work out. If your last marriage was lousy and, like Audrey, you stayed in it a long time even though it was terrible, you will take longer to regain a healthy attitude toward men. Some women are so scarred by terrible marriages that they never remarry. Others are traumatized, but recover enough to forgive and forget, and marry again.

Ruth, age forty, an insurance salesperson, had been single for seven years and couldn't seem to find a new mate. She was cute and peppy and met lots of men through her work, but something always seemed to go wrong with each relationship.

Not finding any common thread in her relationship problems, I asked her about her marriage.

"Oh, that's ancient history, thank God."

She was all too quick to dismiss the subject. Sensing that her feelings about the marriage might be the source of her current problems, I asked her to tell me more. It turned out to be a classic case of marrying earlier, marrying dumber.

"I'd been married two years when I knew for sure it was a terrible marriage. I even had doubts when I walked down the aisle at twenty, but it seemed like the right thing to do at the time. Ron was handsome, well-off, a good catch. All my friends were getting married, so I did too."

Once she started talking about this "ancient history," it all came tumbling out as if it had happened yesterday.

"He was a total dictator, and I was always trying to make him happy. Of course, I couldn't. There wasn't enough I could do. I cooked, I cleaned, I dressed up and entertained, but he always criticized everything I did. Our sex life was terrible. He was too busy screwing every bimbo in town. It was like we weren't even married as far as he was concerned. My friends all felt so sorry for me.

"I stayed in that awful marriage until I was thirty-three. Thirteen long years. If only I'd had the courage to get divorced right away, before we had kids. Once we had the kids, I tried even harder to make him happy, to keep the family together, because my parents were divorced when I was a child and I was determined to keep my kids from going through the same thing I went through. By the time I gave up and got out, I felt like there was nothing I could do to make a man love me."

The first step for Ruth was to figure out what she wanted. Like many women, she only knew what she *didn't* want. "I just never want to feel the way I did before, trapped, stifled, wasting my life. It's tough being a single mother of two kids, but I'll do anything to avoid another marriage like my last one. I'm still prejudiced against guys with blonde hair, or southern accents, or even good physiques—anything that reminds me of Ron."

It was obvious that Ruth's whole life was still under the influence of her bad marriage. Her efforts to build new relationships were being sabotaged by subconscious fears that marriage could destroy her life, causing her to pull away from any man who got close. Instead of figuring out what she wanted in a man, she was still blindly running away from Ron.

Once she'd recognized and admitted how she was being affected by her "ancient history," Ruth could then work on combating its negative effects on her thinking. We started by trying to analyze objectively what was really bad about Ron and what was actually okay about him. After that, we were able to develop some "husband criteria" for Ruth that reflected her current needs, instead of knee-jerk reactions to her past.

Ruth is making good progress. Getting her old negative thoughts in perspective has helped her to trust both herself and a new man in her life. Their relationship has lasted eleven months, and Ruth no longer seems so fearful of remarrying.

Cassandra's first marriage left her scarred in a different way. Brought up in a dirt-poor family, she managed to get an education, worked hard and was able to save a fair amount of money. After she married, her savings provided the down payment for a house where she and her new husband lived. After five years of marriage, they broke up.

"Richard couldn't seem to keep a job. I was sympathetic and willing to help. I said I'd support him while he went to graduate school so he could get an advanced degree and a better job. He simply stayed in graduate school until he was offered an assistant professorship. It didn't pay much—he was really just a professional student—but I figured, 'Well, I married him for richer or poorer, if this is what he wants, okay.' But then I became pregnant, and he began staying away from home more and more.

"He was staying out late, sometimes never coming home. I knew he was having an affair, and when I challenged him, all he had to say was, 'Okay, let's get a divorce.'

"Next thing I know, he's asking for half the house that I'd paid for, plus all my furniture that went into the house, including things I'd inherited from my grandmother that only had sentimental value, and—get this—he wanted me to contribute part of his support since he wasn't quite through with his dissertation yet.

"I couldn't believe the nerve. I had just had the baby, and of course, he couldn't pay child support. He was a child who wanted to be supported.

"It makes me angry whenever I think about what he put me through. I'll never let a man take advantage of me like that again. I'd like to have a warm, nurturing, caring relationship with someone I can trust, but I'm afraid.

"I want a man who will share what he has with me. But all the men I meet seem to have less than I do, or else they're supporting an ex-wife and kids. I don't want the burden for some man's first family to wind up on me. I'm already supporting one child.

"Whenever I meet a man, I worry about his spending habits and whether he would run up big bills on my credit cards like my ex did, or whether he'd get sick and I'd have to support him. I've worked so hard for what I've got, I don't want to lose what little I still have after Richard."

I could empathize with why Cassandra was so worried about losing her money or her house or her belongings. Unfortunately, when she met a new man, she was worse than an IRS auditor, wanting to know how much he made, how secure he was, whether he had any savings or owned any property. Naturally, she was scaring off men by the dozens.

Cassandra was well aware how much she was still affected by her past experience. And her requirement for a man to be financially independent was totally reasonable, given her history. She just needed to keep that requirement in perspective, to remember it was just one of many criteria for a husband.

Cassandra had to begin appreciating the qualities a new man offered instead of looking for what might be wrong with him. She needed to spend some time having fun instead of constantly standing in judgment. In Cassandra's case, a little attitude adjustment and a change in her approach to men worked wonders.

She promised not to mention her bad experience with Richard to new men because it made her sound bitter and defensive. She practiced bringing up financial matters more obliquely, getting the information she wanted from clues during several light conversations rather than demanding direct answers in a nonstop inquisition.

The last time we talked, Cassandra had found a man she was wild about. And he is, as she put it, "not wealthy but financially secure. No problem."

Don't think that a new man is already guilty of whatever the old man did in your life. Remember, start fresh with each new man. Give men a chance to show you who they really are.

When You're a Widow

In some ways, marrying again can be easier for a widow than for a divorced woman. "As a widow, I could do whatever I thought was best for me and for my children," Marjorie told me. Her husband of nineteen years, Kenneth, had died suddenly in an airplane crash.

"I notice that my divorced friends don't have that freedom. No matter what they do, no matter who they marry or where they live, they still have their ex-husbands in their life. He's the father of their children. He's always there. They have to talk to him and get his input on decisions about the kids. They're just not as free."

Marjorie was fortunate. Her attitude toward men was terrific, even when she found herself a widow at forty-five.

"I like men," she said, when she was telling me about David, the new man in her life. "I've always liked men, and when I met David, we simply felt right together. All the love I'd ever felt for Kenneth seemed to be right there, waiting to be tapped again.

"I seemed to trust David right away. I don't know why. It's not that he's just like Kenneth. He's quite different in many ways."

Marjorie was able to trust David so quickly for an important reason: The shock, anger and grief she felt over Kenneth's untimely death didn't undermine her fondness for men and her loving feelings for Kenneth the way a nasty divorce could have. David didn't have to overcome any basic resistance to men or bad memories.

However, some widows whose marriages were wonderfully happy may have a hard time remarrying, especially if they don't remarry soon after their husband's death. Sometimes, each new man is compared to the man they lost. As the years go by, the deceased husband's faults are forgotten and his good traits are made saintly. So the longer a widow waits to remarry, the harder it is for a new man to live up to the man she's lost. Soon no man can ever live up to the cherished memories of her dead hero.

When You Have Children

More than once, loud, angry fights have broken out in my seminars when we discuss what men want and don't want in a marriage. Often, when the men read their lists of what they don't want out loud, their "don't want" list includes women with children. The single mothers in the group become very angry when they hear that men don't want to date women with children, that they prefer childless women. Even though the men are expressing an honest feeling, that they don't want to be instant fathers, women with children are angry, and rightly so.

"What am I supposed to do with my kids?" they want to know. "Strangle them? Hide them? Pretend they don't exist?"

If you have kids, you have to qualify each new man immediately to find out how he feels about kids. Does he like them? Is he at ease with them? Will he like yours? The more difficult your kids are, the harder it will be for you to find a husband. Only a man who's very, very much in love will marry a woman with problem kids.

Some divorced parents use their ex-wives, ex-husbands and children as a way to stay single. After all, as long as they have this insurmountable problem in their lives, they're safe from falling in love.

Gladys, one of my clients, raised her son alone. Her first husband was a ne'er-do-well who is currently homeless. Her second husband was an alcoholic whom she supported. In order to save her son from either fate—homelessness or alcoholism—she has protected him from having to face the world. Now he's twenty-six, still lives at home and is usually surly and insulting to her friends when they visit, especially to Charles, the man in her life.

Charles, it turns out, is also using his children to keep from being able to commit to Gladys or anyone else. He *has* to support two grown daughters through their doctorate degrees. He *has* to help out his ex-wife. There's hardly any money for him, let alone another family. Like many men who avoid commitment in subtle but noticeable ways, Charles' apartment/office is clearly too small for him, and no woman could ever think of moving in there.

Both Gladys and Charles have been upset and angered by each other's inability to deal with their grown children. It stands like a rock between them, always keeping them from dealing with their own relationship. He can't stand being in her house with her son for any length of time, and she can't stay at his cramped apartment for long.

Recently, Gladys' son has started to work regularly and Charles' daughter has gotten a job. Both Gladys and Charles, who have now been dating for seven years in an exclusive relationship, are terrified at the thought that they could be in danger of actually having to commit to each other.

The longer you stay in the "mother-only role," the harder it is for you to imagine yourself in any other. You forget how to be a sex object. You forget what it's like to be adored. Love is like sex. The more you give, the more you have. If you don't give, it fades into a forgotten corner of your life.

When You Have Assets to Protect

You have children and so does your new husband. You each want your individual estates to go to your own children. You're wary of losing what you've got. A premarital agreement can be the best way of handling these matters, but there are real dangers when you try to keep all finances totally separate in a marriage.

When Sylvia and David married, they each had been married twice before. At first, when David, a New Jersey psychiatrist, wanted a prenuptial agreement, Sylvia was mildly annoyed.

"He didn't have a pot to piss in. I had a house. I had investments. I had savings. But he felt like he'd been stripped over the years by his divorces. He lost two houses and felt he'd still have at least one if he'd had prenuptial agreements. So I said okay. I wanted to save my assets separately from his anyway, for my kids. He wanted to do the same.

"Actually, the prenuptial agreement worked out better for me than for him. I thought it would. We keep everything separate. But basically it's not a healthy arrangement. The agreement went too far. We're too separate. We don't share enough.

"When we go out to dinner, he splits the bill. I don't eat that much. I'm a vegetarian, and I don't eat dessert. I always offer to pay my share, and he knows my share is so little it embarrasses him. Nevertheless, he keeps track of everything, and we split it. He's always counting. Actually, he's pretty stingy. He'd be perfectly happy if *I* took *him* out to dinner.

"With everything so separate, I feel as if I'm some kind of room-mate and not his wife. Money is a constant bone of contention.

"I feel that if we shared more, it would make us closer. But I don't feel that I want my money going to pay his alimony or child support."

Agreeing to share and put each other before the kids may be the key to an equitable and comfortable late marriage for older couples.

When Jenny married Maury at age forty-five, she made a much different match than the one she'd made when she was eighteen. Jenny's first marriage, to Oscar, was terrible.

"I was married for twenty-five years the first time to a man with terribly low self-esteem. He constantly put me down to make himself feel like a smarter, more important person than he was. No matter what I did, it was never enough.

"During the marriage, I became a successful entrepreneur, employing 350 women. Oscar earned very little, and when I realized I'd have to feed two kids and he wasn't going to be of much help, I went out and created this business. Even then, after I was making wonderful money, I couldn't do anything right in his eyes. Finally, after twenty-five years of mental abuse, I began to feel better about myself and I got the strength to leave him.

"Meanwhile, I'd known Maury as a friend. We confided in each other and built a bond of friendship. Neither of us could do anything right in our mates' eyes. I knew what to do, my business showed it, but all my husband did was tell me what I was doing wrong. Maury, though, was proud of my accomplishments and praised me.

"I separated from my husband in October. Four months later Maury separated from his wife. At that time I was already dating someone else. When Maury called and asked me out, I told him I was in a relationship. He asked if we could have dinner, just as friends. I said sure, and we went out and had the most wonderful evening. I realized I really cared about him. We started to date, and I dropped the other person.

"We dated for six months and lived together for over a year before we were married. I had been so mentally abused in my first marriage that I suppressed all my feelings. But in my marriage to Maury, we have a lot of trust. We don't hold back anything. We really treasure each other because our past marriages were so difficult.

"Oscar was always telling me what I was doing wrong with my business. I was powerful in business, but I was powerless at home. I know Maury puts me on a pedestal because of my success. He has been to big meetings where I'm the leader, and he loves it.

"It was a challenge to blend our families. But we realized that most of our kids are young adults, ages twenty-one to twenty-five, and we decided to put each other first and our children next. Maury's forty-eight, and his youngest daughter, age fifteen, has just come to live with us. A kid that age is always a challenge. But still, we prioritize each other before anything else.

"Because we put each other first, we've been able to deal with the difficulty of blending families. I see so many second marriages where the kids destroy the relationship. My ex was like living with a cancer that infiltrated my children's brains by making them believe untrue things about me, so I was worried. But the emotions of our kids, actually, weren't much of an obstacle.

"Financially, we decided to blend everything. He has much more property than I do and more money. We take the attitude that we now have four children, not two. We decided to share everything to help us feel more like one.

"My father was intimidating and controlling with my mother, so I thought that same kind of relationship was normal. Now I've made a pact not to settle in life for less than a really loving relationship ever again."

Second Marriages Can Be Better

By now, you know exactly what you didn't like about your first marriage, and you're not about to do that again. You're more sure of who you are than you were when you married the first time, so you stand up for your rights. You won't allow yourself to be swallowed up whole by a man, and you won't allow little discomforts to turn into big divorces. You probe, you challenge, you communicate, you demand real intimacy.

Kay, about to marry at age fifty, looks back at her first marriage and laughs when she realizes how naive she was. "When I married the first time, it was because he was gorgeous. I idolized him. His word was law.

"I remember when he wanted to move to California. I just followed along complacently, dragging two little kids behind. When he wanted to trade in our stationwagon for a Porsche, I didn't say peep. I can't believe how stupid I was that I never spoke up about anything.

"I'll never forget the night we were at the Brown Derby for a romantic dinner. We were looking at the menus by candlelight, and

I looked at him and said, 'Isn't this a wonderful evening? Aren't you happy?' And he said, 'No.'

"I was silent for a second or two, and then, like an idiot, I just said, 'What are you going to order?'

"I wouldn't let something like that go by today. I'd say, 'What's wrong? What can we do about it?' I'm a whole different person now, and so is the man I'm going to marry."

CHAPTER NINETEEN

Children in Later Marriages

When you marry later, the issue of children comes up immediately. Friends don't even wait for the wedding before they start asking, "Are you going to have children?" Having children is often the motivating force behind why you're getting married.

When you're younger, you and your husband just assume you'll eventually have children, but you're not in any rush. When you marry later, the situation is reversed. Having children is not a foregone conclusion, but it is a pressing question. The clock is ticking, your childbearing years are dwindling. Having children is not a question you can postpone. And it's the single biggest incompatibility problem for older couples.

Men Who Want Children

If you're involved with a man who wants children or who you think might want children at some future date and you *don't* want any, you're heading for sure trouble. One of the big dangers for an older woman who marries a younger man is that he'll later decide he wants children.

Men Who Don't Want Children

For older women, especially those marrying for the first time, the problem is usually the opposite: She wants children and he doesn't. A man typically won't want children if (1) he's already had several and (2) he has had a vasectomy.

Deborah, who wanted children desperately, was thirty-eight when she met Darrell, an investment banker with two kids from a previous marriage. "Darrell's kids are only five and eight," she cooed. "I'll mother them. It'll be just like having kids of my own. And who knows, maybe he'll change his mind when he sees how good a mother I am. And men do get their vasectomies reversed, for love," she reminded me. "I bet he'll do it for me."

In spite of my warning to Deborah that caring for Darrell's kids would never be like having kids of her own, Deborah was determined. Before long, Deborah and Darrell got engaged, and I was invited to their wedding.

It was a lovely ceremony with Darrell's children in attendance. Deborah was ecstatic. Then, when Deborah turned forty, she decided she couldn't wait any longer. Her timeclock was running out, and by then, she had discovered the truth about being a stepparent. "It's just not the same. They have a mother. They treat me like a good friend, but not at all like a mother. The problem is that Darrell went crazy when I talked to him about it."

Soon they were in my office together, both feeling angry, upset and threatened. Deborah felt Darrell was being insensitive and intransigent. Darrell felt betrayed. And each felt the other was being unreasonable. Darrell sounded adamant.

"Dammit, I've had all the kids I ever want. I told you that before we got married and you agreed. I didn't force you, you agreed willingly!"

"Darrell, I've tried," Deborah replied tearfully. "I've tried so hard to be happy mothering your kids. I just didn't know it wouldn't be the same." She turned to me for support.

"Tracy, tell him, this has nothing to do with agreements or logic. It's biological. I'm overwhelmed with this need to have a child, to pass on my genes or something. It haunts me. Every time I see your kids, Darrell, it just makes me want my own child more. I'm sorry, but this is a big hurt, a giant hole in my life. Don't you understand? God, I feel like I'm ruining my whole life by not trying for motherhood right now! I'm so unhappy."

Darrell became less strident, but still firm. "I hear you. I feel bad for you. I hate to see you so unhappy. But the idea of having more kids at this point in our lives is crazy. Jesus, I'm forty-six. I'd be over sixty when our kids would be in their teens."

"Oh, Darrell, I'd do all the work. We can afford help."

"Deb, you could never keep up with a two-year-old. They're into everything. And if the kid's going to be brought up by a nanny, what's the point?"

There was no solution. Deborah decided to stick with Darrell and get as much satisfaction as possible from her stepchildren. But deep down, the ache never went away.

In my years of counseling couples, I've found that love and compromise can solve almost any relationship problem—with one exception: I've never figured out how half of a couple can be a parent and the other half not be.

If a man doesn't want children and you do, there's usually no compromise position. Having children is a yes or no decision. You can't have children just a little bit or for just a little while.

Rule for Childless Women

If you've never had children, don't ever agree to forego them. I don't care how you feel about children right now. Even if you're sure you only want your career and a husband. Even if you're totally cynical about kids, the mothering urge can blindside you, hit you like a runaway train with no warning. You can go all through your thirties relishing your freedom, smug about having escaped the hassles and responsibilities of kids. Then, suddenly, you wake up one morning and everything's changed. You start melting whenever you see a baby. You envy mothers taking their kids to school. You feel empty, despairingly unfulfilled. You *need* to have a baby—and you definitely don't want to be in Deborah's shoes at that point.

How Late Is Too Late to Be a Mother?

Women put off having children for a host of reasons—some because they want to get their careers launched first, some because they don't marry until later, some because they just don't feel the mothering urge until later. How late is it safe to wait?

Almost ten percent of all women are infertile to begin with. If you are healthy and fertile, your ability to bear children starts to decrease rapidly starting in your late thirties. From forty to fifty, the clock runs out.

> At age forty, twenty percent of women are unable to get pregnant.
>
> At age forty-five, sixty percent of women are unable to get pregnant.
>
> At age forty-seven, or forty-eight, seventy-five to ninety percent of women can't get pregnant.
>
> At age fifty, only ten percent can get pregnant.

Advances in medical science have made childbearing far safer for older mothers, but first, you have to get pregnant. If you don't have a husband with a high sperm count, what are your options?

Sperm Banks

Whether you're married or not, the least expensive way to get a baby is to have your own. Even if your husband has had a vasectomy or a very low sperm count, you can get sperm from a sperm bank such as Idant Lab in New York. Dr. Joseph Feldschuh of Idant says they're responsible for 14,500 births around the world. Idant will send sperm to your own gynecologist, or if you go to New York directly to the lab, you can be artificially inseminated there for around $100, including sperm.

The sperm at Idant comes from college students and is guaranteed AIDS free. It's frozen for three months after it's donated, and the donor is tested each month.

Almost any woman, married or not, is eligible for artificial insemination at Idant Sperm Bank, but she must be emotionally and financially stable. Single women without jobs are usually rejected. "We don't want the mother and child to wind up on welfare," says Dr. Feldschuh.

Here's how it works at Idant: Your doctor will send Idant a description of your husband, and the sperm bank will try to match his description with a donor. You also can choose by the graduate student donor's major academic and athletic achievements.

"The general characteristics of the child can be chosen," explains Dr. Feldschuh, "but we don't suggest trying to choose a certain sex. You can greatly increase your chance of getting a boy, for example, but you lose ninety-five percent of the sperm in the process, so your overall chance of getting pregnant is decreased.

"I'm all for having more intelligent kids. We certainly try for very intelligent donors. It's not unusual for a couple to return and have two or even three children by the same donor.

"We encourage the second and third children from the same father so that they're natural siblings. Donors don't stay around forever donating sperm, so we inform the woman how much of her donor's sperm is left. She can store it if she thinks she might want more children at a later date. It only costs fifty-five dollars for the sperm and ten dollars to store it for a year.

"We were the first to do AIDS testing. We also test for hepatitis and HIV-I, and AIDS-related virus. Seventy-five percent of women are successful at getting pregnant within three months, assuming they don't have any physical problems, that they're producing good eggs, that their womb is intact and that their endocrine system is operating."

When Lynn and Clifford married, Clifford had already had children.

"I was thirty-four and Clifford was forty. He already had three kids from his previous marriage, eight-year-old twins and a nine-year-old. He'd had a vasectomy." Lynn picked at her fingers nervously as she talked to me in my office.

"After eight years of marriage, I was desperate to have a child. Clifford and I had stipulated as part of our agreement to get married that we'd have one child. But when it came time for me to do it or else, he changed his mind and said he didn't want to after all. He'd had it with fatherhood. His kids were nothing but trouble. He was just relieved that they were almost grown, and he didn't want to start over again.

"He bought me a dog, a golden retriever puppy, hoping it would be a substitute. When the dog didn't deter my desire for a baby, he began to hate the dog. Now he's mean to the dog, and I feel guilty.

"Anyway, the dog didn't satisfy me. I became more and more determined. I couldn't bide my time anymore, so I began to insist he get a vasectomy reversal or that I get artificial insemination.

"He was really upset. 'You have no idea what having a small child is like. It'll change our lives. We won't be able to travel. I'm almost fifty. I'll be ready to retire soon. Besides, I've had my vasectomy for many years. They tied the ends. I don't think it can be reversed.'

"So I said I'd just get artificially inseminated. He could come with me and help me pick out the father of our child. He became furious. 'You mean you'd actually have another man's child?' he kept saying. 'Just what I want to do, spend the rest of my life raising some other man's child.' I didn't know what to say, but I knew I had to have this child, even if it meant I'd lose my marriage.

"Clifford finally agreed to the vasectomy reversal, but he said if we had a child, it was to be totally my responsibility. He didn't want anything to do with it. His vasectomy reversal was very difficult and painful for him. Afterwards, I didn't get pregnant and wound up having artificial insemination after all.

"Then I got pregnant with twins. Clifford went crazy. One baby was bad enough. Two was going to be the end of the world. Even though I pointed out that we could afford lots of help, nannies, babysitters, the works, he was miserable.

"When the babies came, he was distant. He didn't help. He didn't get involved with them at all. The whole situation was difficult for us.

"Now the babies are almost two years old, and he's starting to come around. But he's going to be fifty-two this year, and he's having trouble feeling good about being the father of these two little boys. When people see them together, they say, 'Oh what cute grandchildren you have.'

"But I feel like these babies are here forever. Something could happen to him. Our marriage could break up. But that could have happened anyway. This way, no matter what happens, I have my babies."

Unfortunately, not all artificial inseminations work, and after many tries, some couples will have to face the far higher cost of a surrogate or an adoption.

Surrogates

Noel Keane is perhaps the most well-known surrogate parenting lawyer in the United States. Keane's surrogates have given birth to 275 babies, there are 44 on the way, and 200 couples have chosen surrogates and are in the process.

At his Infertility Centers in New York and Las Vegas and at his law office in Michigan, Keane, who serves a growing population of later brides and infertile couples, says: "They can't very well adopt if they're older because in adoption there's the unwritten "forty-to-one rule." This means neither you nor your husband can be more than forty years older than the child you want to adopt. Even with private adoptions, the couple has to pass a "home study," and the social worker who does the home study can simply declare them too old. Some jurisdictions are different in different parts of the country, so I advise couples to try to find a jurisdiction that doesn't enforce the age rule as strictly.

"The good part of surrogate parenting is that a man can be a father at any age. Chief Justice Douglas became a father at seventy-six. In a surrogate situation, the father doesn't have to adopt the child because it's already his—he's already the biological father. And no one is going to do 'home studies' on you. We've even had one surrogate in vitro birth where the donor egg provider and the sperm provider were declared parents, not the birth mother." The total cost, should you and your husband want to hire a surrogate through Keane, is currently around $35,000. This includes $16,000 for the center, $10,000 for the surrogate, plus screening doctors, psychologist, adoption costs and insemination fees. If your husband has a low sperm count, his sperm can be mixed with sperm from a donor. Then nobody really knows who the father is, and your husband can be the legal father. Any man who consents to his wife's being artificially inseminated can be acknowledged as the child's father.

Adoptions

Now that birth mothers have discovered how much financial support they can get, adoption isn't as inexpensive as it once was. The demand for healthy babies and the financial need of birth mothers has created a symbiotic relationship between the adoptive parents who want a baby and the birth mothers.

The mutual need is obvious, and birth mothers who were once quietly ashamed for bearing a child "out of wedlock" are now openly negotiating to get the best deal for themselves and their unborn children. They are in demand. They have a scarce commodity—babies.

You have the option to adopt, depending on your age and the age of your husband. If you're both thirty-eight or under, and if you're willing to take an older child (five years or more), and if you're willing to take a mixed-race child or a sick or handicapped child, you may be able to get a child through the regular public adoption routes. That's a lot of "if's," and you still must be prepared to wait, perhaps for years, and pass intensive investigation and scrutiny.

In most cases, older couples wind up going to a private adoption lawyer like Leslie Slatter of Slatter & Slatter in Los Angeles. That's where Jean and Mark, both thirty-eight, found their baby girl Jenna.

"It was like a miracle. Only three months from the time we contacted Leslie's office, we had a healthy, Caucasian, blue-eyed, blonde-haired baby girl.

"I couldn't seem to get pregnant even though I tried, and finally we found out my husband had practically a zero sperm count. Then we tried artificial insemination for a year and it didn't take, so adoption seemed right for me. We could have kept trying, but being a family was more important to me that having a baby biologically, so we decided to adopt.

"When we tried public adoption, we were told we'd have to wait five years, even for an older child. We would be in a long line of couples, and there would be no guarantees as to how long it would take.

"We even thought of adopting in South America, but the requirements sometimes mean you have to establish residency there to adopt. I just couldn't take that kind of time off from work, so a foreign adoption became impossible. Private adoption was our obvious choice.

"Our birth mother didn't contact a lawyer until three weeks before the birth. She had her own medical insurance, so we didn't have any medical expenses. Our costs were still $8000 for everything, but we're gloriously happy with our child. I'd love to go back to the same parents again and adopt another one.

"Our lawyer was herself an adoptive mother. My husband had been an adopted child. We all felt comfortable with adoption."

Slatter & Slatter, like many private adoption lawyers, only handles open adoptions. Public-agency adoptions are more likely to be closed adoptions, which means the birth mother and the adopting parents never have any contact. In an open adoption, an arrangement is made for the birth mother to have some ongoing communication with the adoptive parents.

"Ours is through the lawyer," Jean continued. "We send pictures and a letter once a year. We were there when our daughter was born, and we know the mother and the father.

"I'd advise women to get tests done right away if they don't get pregnant, not wait like I did. Also, talk to people about adoption. You'll be surprised at how many have been adopted or have adopted children. After you adopt, it seems like everyone has some experience with adoption.

"Also, when you adopt, don't be fussy. Even with private adoption, the fussier you are, the longer you wait. If you're not concerned about the situation, if you're willing to take a mixed-race child, it's easier.

"We didn't know the race of the father until we saw him in the delivery room. But we were flexible, open-minded and relaxed, even though we heard from the lawyer about the child only thirty-six hours before she was delivered. We had to get ready in a hurry.

"It really takes a lawyer to deal with birth mothers. They don't always walk in and say here are the facts. Often they can't make up their mind about keeping the baby. Sometimes they lie about the baby's father. Sometimes they don't know. They have to be tested for drugs. The lawyer has to find out how prenatal care has been, gather data on the mother's health, have various medical tests run."

If you are really determined to have a child, and you have unlimited financial resources, you can probably become a mother at any age. However, if you lack the money for a surrogate and/or your husband is too old or won't support your application for adoption, you're back to having your own baby. And here, although the options for healthy sperm are limitless, you're totally subject to that inexorable biological timeclock.

CHAPTER TWENTY

Merging Lifestyles

When Marshall and I moved in together, we almost didn't make it through day one. Moving day was traumatic. Marshall, who enjoys cooking and likes a well-organized kitchen, kept opening drawers in the kitchen and asking, "What's this stuff?" Each time I would say, "Oh, that's my junk drawer." I hadn't had anyone open my drawers and give me that look since I was fourteen.

Merging Households

I had vaguely figured on clearing out maybe one closet and a chest of drawers for his clothes. I hadn't realized that making room for his clothes, desk, computer, pictures, books, sporting equipment and miscellaneous favorite things would involve reorganizing the whole house. Since I'd never been married, I didn't know how much space a man needed, how much room a man can take up in your life.

I quickly found out. As the moving men kept carrying in carton after carton, I had to keep rethinking my space planning. Again and again I would find myself looking at a huge space-wasting piece of antique furniture that was decorative but definitely in the way and

219

thinking, "Do I want this piece of furniture in my life, or do I want Marshall in my life?" I always chose Marshall.

Even so, there really wasn't room for everything we both brought to our marriage. Belongings his daughters had left in his old house, things my brother had left in mine. Tons of books. Some are still in boxes in our garage, almost ten years later. Merging households can be a major production when you bring along all the baggage from previous lifetimes.

If possible, the two of you should move into a new home together. That way, neither of you feels as if you're crowding into the other's space. Also, you won't feel like you're sleeping where oh-so-many others have gone before.

Dealing with In-Laws

When you marry a man, you don't just marry him, you marry his entire family as well, even if they're not at all in evidence prior to your marriage. Especially his parents. Marrying later means you marry a man whose parents are retired, maybe quite elderly.

This means that they're less likely to be popping in on you all the time. Older people often don't travel well and don't want their routines interrupted. Your new in-laws may very well be living in one of those out-of-the-way retirement communities in Arizona or Florida, where they're happy and content to stay.

Regardless of age or location, don't expect your new mother-in-law to welcome you with open arms. The man's mother is usually much more of a problem than the woman's mother. Since the caveman days, the man dragged his woman back to his cave where she had to fit in, rather than the other way around. It's anthropological.

When a younger woman marries, she's more flexible, more subservient and more likely to be able to get along with her mother-in-law. You, on the other hand, are none of the above. And don't count on your new mother-in-law to be a pushover either, just because she's old and frail. I've heard some real horror stories from some of my older women clients.

If your husband-to-be has never been married before, his mother can be very possessive and jealous. She won't feel that she's gaining a daughter, she'll feel that you're taking her son away. After all, she's been the only woman in his life for many years, the apple of his eye, and now you've taken over as his number one woman.

If your husband-to-be has been married before, then she'll see you as one in a string of hussies who don't deserve her wonderful son.

If you've been married before, she'll suspect you're a wicked divorcée.

If you've been on vacation together before, she'll think you're a tramp.

If you live with the man before you marry him, she'll be sure you're a tramp.

If you've never been married before, she'll think it's because nobody wanted you because you're a sex maniac or frigid or psychopathic.

If you're so sweet butter wouldn't melt in your mouth, she'll just be suspicious.

Often, perseverance pays in winning over a man's mother, so be nice. Try hard.

If your mother-in-law absolutely, positively refuses to respond pleasantly to you, limit the time you have to be around your in-laws. Negotiate. "One Christmas with your family, one with mine."

If your new mother-in-law totally rejects you, just stay out of her way; it's a battle you'll never win. Meanwhile, encourage your husband to visit his parents by himself, so you don't come between him and his family in any way.

If you do have the good fortune to have a mother-in-law who thinks it's wonderful that you're marrying her son, appreciate her. She's a rare commodity.

His Ex-Wife

It pays to cultivate some degree of friendship with his ex, even if there are no children involved. After all, you can consult her whenever your spouse does something you don't like, to find out if he's pulling something new or if he always did it.

Maybe she'll tell you how she handled his uncontrollable need for an airplane. Maybe she's got a formula to keep him from spending all his time at his computer or his model trains. Or maybe she can save you the aggravation of trying and assure you he went into deep depression whenever he was separated from his model trains for any length of time.

His Friends

Not all his old friends are going to be thrilled that he's marrying you. Some of the women will refuse to be friends with both of you. And you may find that you don't enjoy the company of his good buddies at all.

If possible, include his friends in social events, parties, dinners and so on. But don't expect them to love you the way they love him. After all, they have years of history with him, not with you. And they probably know a different side of your new husband than you do. If you find you can't stand your husband's old buddies, don't despair. You don't have to see them very often, if at all. Encourage him to spend time with them, though, even if you don't want to. That way he won't think you're taking his friends away.

Your Friends

You've known some of your friends since grammar school. Of course, they're going to be a part of your new life with your new husband, or so you think. What a big surprise you're in for when you bring them together.

They don't have a history of memories together. They each care for you, but don't be surprised if they're jealous and suspicious of each other. There you are, having a nice evening together, when suddenly your best friend and your husband are at each other's throats.

"He's just a nasty bully!" she cries on her way out the door.

"Did you hear what she said? That know-it-all bitch!" he complains to you after she's left.

And you wonder if you will ever be able to have your new husband and your best friend in the same room together. There's a good chance they'll get used to each other, but it may take some time.

You've had years to get to love your friend's idiosyncrasies. You've always been able to see your friend's good side. But to your husband, she's the person you talk to on the phone when he wants your attention. She's the one who's sitting in your living room having tea when he comes home and wants to be alone with you. Until your hubby and best friend learn to appreciate each other, you may have to continue spending time with her in off-hours, when your husband is busy continuing his friendship with his male chauvinist buddy you can't stand.

If your best friend is married or has a steady boyfriend, it's probably going to be even harder for you because you now have four people who all have to like each other instead of three.

If your best friend is single, she's going to need lots of extra attention, which you won't have time to give. You're going to feel pressured and pulled in different directions, and she's going to feel as if you've left her for a stranger.

Still-Romantic Ex-Lovers

The best way to handle ex-lovers who "just want to stay friends" is with a simple policy. Whether they're your ex-lovers or his, let them know that if they want to be friends, they have to be friends with *both* of you. If an ex invites you to lunch at a romantic restaurant, say, "Bob and I do things together. Why don't you bring a date, and we'll make it a foursome?"

Finances

Many couples make the mistake of not dealing with financial matters until after they're married. Full disclosure of finances should take place before you get married. This means freely and openly discussing outstanding obligations or debts either of you may have, including alimony and child support, deciding whether your earnings and investments will be pooled or kept separate and agreeing on a preliminary household budget.

If neither of you has very much in the way of assets, you'll probably just agree to share whatever you both make in the future. Couples who agree to share have the fewest fights about money.

If one of you is coming into the marriage with a lot more property than the other one, you may want to consult a lawyer regarding a prenuptial agreement to keep your previously acquired property out of the community-property pool.

If one or both of you have children from former marriages, you may want to set aside certain assets for your children. In this case as well, you should see a lawyer to make the necessary arrangements before you get married.

If you decide to go into the marriage with separate assets for any reason, at least set up a joint household and living account. That way you're not always trying to allocate expenses between "his" and "hers" down to the last parking attendant tip, and may the best accountant win.

Working Out Differences

He may have preconceived ideas about how your vacations should be taken, how often you should go out to dinner or how your money should be spent. He also may have some definite ideas about who does what—who balances the checkbook, who handles the money, who handles the cooking, who takes out the trash and who takes care of the garden. Not to mention who should be romantic and when and who should initiate sex and how.

Changing any of his preconceived ideas can take time and patience. It took me three years to convince Marshall that an early dinner was healthier.

Talk about these issues together, and learn to negotiate to get what you want. For instance, my idea of a vacation is to keep moving from place to place, sightseeing. Marshall likes to find a great place and then stay there. We learned to compromise, doing some of each.

After you've been with your man for a while, you begin to know what things will start a fight. With my husband, all I have to do is criticize his driving. That's guaranteed to start a battle. Knowing how to set him off means I have a choice—to fight or not. You too will have a choice in your relationship. Be aware when you choose to start a fight.

Men hate to be blamed for anything. So if you want to avoid fighting, don't blame your husband; blame an inanimate object. For example, instead of saying, "You still haven't fixed the leaky faucet," say, "The faucet's still leaking."

Learn to negotiate. If you want something from him, make it in his interest to do what you want. Instead of saying, "How about going out to dinner?" try, "If you take me out to dinner, I'll go to the ballgame with you next week."

Be realistic enough to know that no two people live together in this world without problems. So when problems come up, work them out. If you get stuck, see a therapist. Get help before little problems become big ones. In this way, your later marriage will be your last marriage as well.

When you marry later, your expectations are more realistic. You realize that having a good relationship is more important than always being right. Most of all, you value the love you've found much more because you know what life is like without it.

CHAPTER TWENTY-ONE

Keeping Love Alive

Right now, you're both in love. But what about the future? What can you do today to ensure that your new hubby stays in love with you? More than you think.

Maintaining Harmony

A simple way to keep harmony in your relationship is to emphasize the areas in which you agree with each other, the things that are alike about you instead of what's different. Begin by getting in tune with your husband again.

Soon his unconscious will get the message that the two of you are really alike, really one, really together. His subconscious will send a message of harmony to his conscious mind, and he will be drawn to you.

Showing Your Love

It's not just teenagers who worry about being cool. Some grown-ups seem to have the same need for peer approval, always acting

226

so sophisticated. They never show affection in public and never, ever say "I love you" when they call home from the office.

From all my work in counseling couples, I've made a simple observation: If a couple is in trouble, they don't touch a lot and they don't say "I love you" a lot. On the other hand, whenever a couple is doing both, I've found their relationship to be solid.

So the hell with being cool. I say hug a lot, kiss a lot and say "I love you" all the time. Not just at home, but also when you're in public. People may stare, but they'll probably go home and surprise their own spouse with an extra big hug. That is, if they have a spouse. Be happy you do. Show it.

Don't just touch him when you're feeling lovey-dovey and he's behaving like a prince. Even if he's angry about something, standing there grumping at you, *especially* then, go over to him, hug him and interrupt his tirade with a sweet "I love you." Sound crazy? Just try it.

Creating Romantic Triggers

You can set the stage for a lasting love relationship by using romantic triggers to keep love alive. You can then use these same triggers later, to bring back love's spark when it begins to fade.

You probably already have romantic triggers—a favorite piece of music you refer to as "our song" is a common example. Unfortunately, all too many couples stop playing "their" song. It's kind of embarrassing, after you're old marrieds, to play something that reminds you of how "mushy" you were or how silly you may have acted, right?

Well, that's exactly why you *should* play it. The song is more than a reminder, stronger than a memory. That song is a love trigger, with the power to embarrass you with the intensity of the feelings you had when you were most romantic. How? By almost physically connecting you with those feelings.

Other things that are special to you now are worth preserving and using as love triggers later. Stock up on the special perfume he's crazy about right now. It might go out of fashion, but never for him. The same applies to that special after-shave he always wears that you love. And the pet names you have for each other now are not just for the "in love" phase—keep using them. Friends may tease you, saying you sound corny or cutesy. They're just jealous.

If you don't have any triggers, start some. Is there a special way you always touch a certain part of his body, a tiny kiss on his ear, the way you touch his hair? If not, begin thinking ahead.

When the man you love is having a good time, reach out, touch him in a special way. Say "I love you" or something special and sweet. Then, next time you want to get him into a romantic mood, just reach out, touch the same spot, say the words, and voilà, you've tapped into his prior loving feelings.

Your wedding day, the most romantic day of your life, provides endless opportunities to create romantic triggers you can draw on later. Your wedding album is an obvious example, but there are many other ways to set up other specific triggers, so that years later your wedding is more than a distant memory.

Right now, as you plan your wedding, think ahead. Plan to frame a special wedding picture or your invitation in a prominent place in your home as a constant reminder of the way you feel about each other now. If you can possibly afford it, have a video made of your special day.

We watch our wedding video each year on our wedding anniversary. It never fails to make us feel as romantic as the day we were married.

Be sure that lots of your favorite music will be played at your wedding, so you'll be able to play that same music—a whole collection of "your songs"—anytime later, and subconsciously, you and your mate will be connected to the loving feelings you both had that day.

Your honeymoon experience can be another romantic trigger that will last forever. Let's say you spend your honeymoon in Hawaii. The sound of Hawaiian music, the smell of tropical flowers, the scent of suntan lotion, a sunset at the beach, even the sound of the waves breaking can all be future romantic triggers.

For instance, your husband has been grumpy all week, and you're in the mood for a little romance. You put on your Hawaiian Pikake perfume, softly play your favorite Hawaiian music and serve him a tropical drink. And guess what? His subconscious mind starts to remind him of the warm and wonderful romantic feelings he had on your honeymoon. His grumpy feelings start to disappear, and his romantic memories take over.

Using Your Love Triggers

No one's love can be constant through leaky toilets, crying babies, demanding families, business problems and bank overdrafts. Every relationship has its ups and downs, and no two people live together without having problems.

Your accumulated love triggers are there to be used. Your wedding album has the power to bring back very intense loving feelings—but only if you look at it. Many wedding albums just gather dust on a shelf.

In my practice, I counsel lots of couples who used to be in love but now have serious problems. Often they have powerful love triggers that are buried, and all the couple needs is to make contact with them again. Doug and Danielle, married twelve years, were already in trouble when they came to me.

"What do you do to keep him in love?" I asked Danielle. "Nothing lately," Doug growled.

"Neither have you," Danielle retorted. So I asked them to think back and remember when they used to be in love, to picture where they were, what they were doing, what they said. Instantly, their angry expressions softened.

"Tell me what life was like for you then," I asked them.

"We lived at the marina in Ventura then," Danielle began remembering. "We had a boat, and we walked on the beach a lot."

"I used to fish," Doug chimed in. "And each evening, we'd sit on the deck of the boat and have cocktails and watch the sunset." They looked directly at each other and smiled, for the first time, remembering.

I encouraged them to begin taking little weekend trips together to Ventura. They were to make no demands on each other. They didn't have to make love or even talk nice if they didn't want to. All they were to do was to go back to the same place.

At first, they were uncomfortable with each other, but the discomfort only lasted a short time. Soon, the weekend trips became more frequent, and they were beginning to enjoy each other again. Just being around the smell of saltwater had rekindled romantic memories for both of them. In only a few months they were back together. Now they've sold their house in Encino and have moved to Ventura, and they've fallen madly in love with each other again.

All good marriages include a special reservoir of love—a private pool of memories, ongoing affection, shared joys and loving feelings. It's a most unusual reservoir. The more you draw on it, the deeper it gets. The less you draw on it, the more it shrinks. If you never tap into it, it can dry up.

So whenever the present doesn't live up to the best of your past, don't forget your secret reservoir of love. Draw on it, freely and deeply—even if love's the furthest thing from your mind. *Especially* if love's the furthest thing from your mind.

Love's Magic

In really good marriages, where couples have openly demonstrated their love for each other and have frequently tapped into their reservoir of love triggers and memories, I hear the same, amazing thing from the older husbands: "When I look at my wife, I don't see white hair and wrinkles, I see the woman I fell in love with, just as I always have."

Marrying Later,
Marrying Smarter
WORKBOOK

I'm looking for a mate who ...

He'll be lucky to get me because I ...

If a man gives me ...
I would put up with ...

A man is out of my life if he ...

♡ **As a Way of Evaluating a Man, Answer the Following Questions About Him**

_____ Does he get along with his family?

_____ Does he love his mother, sisters, brothers, etc.?
　　　If not, why not?

_____ Does his family love him?
　　　If not, why not?

_____ Does he have a violent temper?

_____ Does he drink or take drugs?

_____ Does he lie, cheat or steal?

_____ Does he take care of his health?

_____ Does he get along with his ex'es?

_____ Is he close to his children?

_____ Does he have long-standing friendships?

_____ Does he pay his bills?

_____ Is he so tied up with his work, hobbies, old buddies or sports that he has little time for you?

_____ Is he willing to make time for you?

_____ Can you take him around your family?

_____ Does he want to be married?

_____ Is he mean to you?

_____ Does he yell at you?

_____ Does he criticize you and/or your friends?

_____ Does he mooch off you?

_____ Does he pay his share?

_____ Do you feel like you're walking on eggs?

_____ Are you always afraid he'll leave?

_____ Can you depend on him to be where he says he's going to be and do what he says he'll do when he says he'll do it?

_____ Would you trust him to feed your pets while you were on a business trip?

_____ Does he appreciate you? Does he say so?

_____ Would you consider spending the rest of your life with him?

_____ Is he okay, just the way he is?

♡ **As a Way of Analyzing Your Past Relationships, Answer Each of the Following Questions About the Relationship**

Were you able to commit?

Was he able to commit?

Were you ready to commit?

Was he ready to commit?

What fantasies of yours did he fill?

What fantasies of his did you fill?

What didn't he like about you?

What didn't you like about him?

If you've been involved with men who weren't able or ready to commit, begin choosing men who are definitely ready to marry. You've been choosing men with other priorities. If you haven't been ready or able to commit, then you've been choosing men you wouldn't marry. Choosing unavailable men is a good way to avoid commitment.

If you discover that the men you've had relationships with just didn't fill your fantasies or you didn't fill theirs, you haven't been choosing from among men who want you. You probably haven't been choosing either. Begin to choose men who meet your requirements and you will dramatically increase your odds of marrying.

♡ Was the Timing Right?

We were happy for [how long]?

We made love [how long after meeting]?

I fell in love with his ...

He fell in love with my ...

In the beginning, I felt ...

In the middle, I felt ...

In the end, I felt ...

Years afterward, I felt ...

I still feel ...

I always wanted him to ...

He always wanted me to ...

If you weren't happy in the relationship very long and/or you stayed in the relationship long after the good times were over, you can see how much time you've wasted. Stop wasting time on relationships in which you're not happy. Either work out the problems or move on.

Follow the "seventy percent rule." If you're not happy seventy percent of the time, get out.

♡ Were the Feelings Right?

When we made love, I felt ...

When we were apart, I felt ...

When we were together, I felt ...

I was afraid he would ...

I wish he could have ...

I wish he didn't ...

I always worried about ...

We never had enough ...

♡ Did You Give Away Too Much Power?

I always felt stronger/weaker.

At first, I was the active pursuer/the pursued.

In the middle, I was the pursuer/pursued.

In the end, I was the pursuer/pursued.

I was always the one who held on/let go.

I was the giver/taker.

I was the wise one/the fool.

I was the caretaker/the cared for.

I was sexually aggressive/sexually passive.

I was in charge/out of control.

I was leaned on/supported.

I was the talker/the silent one.

I was the fighter/the one who gave in.

If you've always felt like the underdog in your relationships, the cure is to choose only from among men who really want you. If you've always been the victim, stop telling men how other men have victimized you in the past. That way you won't set yourself up to be victimized. You'll stop attracting victimizers.

If you've always been the weaker person in the relationship, stop eating your anger. Practice telling men when you don't like something. Take responsibility for getting what you want. Practice telling men what you want. Listen to your feelings. When you don't feel right about doing something, don't do it.

♡ Evaluating a Current Relationship

Do you see each other on a regular basis?

Does he call when he says he will?

Does he make dates into the future?

Do you have future plans together?

Are you spending more time together?

Have you met his parents?

Has he met your family?

Does he get along with your friends, children, pets?

Does he say he loves you?

Have you discussed finances?

Are you happy at least seventy percent of the time?

♡ Lists for Evaluating a Man

WHAT YOU MUST HAVE:

WHAT YOU CAN'T STAND:

HIS ASSETS:

HIS LIABILITIES:

If you have any questions and would like to reach Dr. Cabot, write to The Relationship Research Institute, P.O. Box 3544, Van Nuys, CA 91407.